HOW TO

GARDEN INDOORS

& Grow Your Own Food Year Round

Ultimate Guide to Vertical, Container, and Hydroponic Gardening

KIM ROMAN

CRE🏠TIVE
HOMEOWNER®

Dedication

This book is dedicated to my grandchildren: Katelyn Falk, Luther Falk, and Reece Roman; my sons: Jeremy Roman and Matthew Roman; my daughter-in-law, Crystal Roman; and my husband, MSgt Tim Roman, USAF, retired. Family is everything!

Special Thanks

My sincerest thanks to Katie Elzer-Peters of *TheGardenOfWords.com* and Shawna Coronado of *ShawnaCoronado.com* for believing in me. Also, to Catoctin Mountain Park for allowing us to take photos at historic Camp Misty Mount in Thurmont, Maryland. If you're looking for unique volunteer opportunities, try *www.Volunteer.gov*. Very special thank yous go out to my multi-talented daughter-in-law, Crystal Roman, of *www.CrystalRomanPhotography.com*, and Guy DiRoma, who kept me in check and sane along the way.

CREATIVE
HOMEOWNER®

How to Garden Indoors & Grow Your Own Food Year Round
Editor: Colleen Dorsey
Designer: Freire Disseny + Comunicació, Llara Pazdan
Indexer: Jay Kreider

ISBN 978-1-58011-867-5 (paperback)
ISBN 978-1-58011-574-2 (hardcover)
ISBN 978-1-58011-577-3 (spiral)

Library of Congress Control Number: 2021938131

We are always looking for talented authors. To submit an idea, please send a brief inquiry to acquisitions@foxchapelpublishing.com.

Printed in China
Second printing

Creative Homeowner®, *www.creativehomeowner.com*, is an imprint of New Design Originals Corporation and distributed exclusively in North America by Fox Chapel Publishing Company, Inc., 800-457-9112, 903 Square Street, Mount Joy, PA 17552, and in the United Kingdom by Grantham Book Service, Trent Road, Grantham, Lincolnshire, NG31 7XQ.

Foreword

As we climb our way out of the pandemic, it certainly has left us with some great opportunities. An understanding of food insecurity has now become "mainstream" and not just for those living in food deserts. Not only city dwellers, but also those in suburban areas, saw empty produce shelves. Where would we get fresh food if our supply chains were cut? How would we feed our families? Through adversity, new ideas are born, and old ones can suddenly make even more sense.

Kim Roman learned long ago through her work with Mel Bartholomew, the founder and creator of Square Foot Gardening™ and the SFG Foundation, that thinking outside the box can result in solutions to real-world problems. Having become a Square Foot Gardening Certified Instructor in 2010, Kim not only worked directly with Mel, but also worked closely with the Square Foot Gardening Foundation on our national best-selling gardening book, *All New Square Foot Gardening, 3rd Edition*. Her input has been invaluable.

Kim's passion is finding ways to solve hunger by working in her suburban community and in the inner cities in the state of Maryland, where she resides, and around the world. With her extensive gardening knowledge, she is making real inroads in teaching people with limited resources how to feed themselves. Thousands of new gardeners under her tutelage as a Square Foot Gardening Certified Instructor are now equipped to grow nutritious food as a result.

As one of our top Certified Instructors, Kim is helping us further our mission around the world to help end world hunger "one square foot at a time." She walks the walk by working with at-risk youth, the homeless, victims of sexual exploitation, veterans, and those who have limited access to healthy produce. Some of the organizations Kim has worked with include World Relief (an international and development agency), Gardens for Heroes (which provides gardens for wounded veterans and their caregivers), and The Samaritan Women in Baltimore (which helps to provide housing for victims of sexual exploitation), just to name a few.

With her years of research and hands-on application in the field, Kim has gained extensive insights into the needs of others and how to tackle finding real solutions—so much so that the SFG Foundation named Kim an official SFG Ambassador to our mission and method. This accolade is given only to the most valued and experienced Certified SFG Instructors, as they play an important role in providing advice and strategic guidance to the Foundation. Kim, with the help of the Square Foot Gardening Foundation, traveled to Africa with her home church (Abundant Life Church, Glen Burnie, Maryland) and taught SFG and composting at a remote church in Kenya with *Convoy of Hope*. She taught them the principles of composting and how to grow their own food. Think of how many of those villagers can now teach others to help themselves and how that knowledge can expand and change lives.

We are so proud and excited that Kim has written *How to Garden Indoors & Grow Your Own Food Year Round* to help people grow nutritious, healthy food indoors. This thorough guide will no doubt encourage countless readers that they can grow their own food in limited space or in a cold climate.

In these unknown times, and by thinking outside the box, Kim guides her readers in a fun, easy way that includes lots of tips, fresh new ideas, photos, and real "how-to" practical learning for growing food indoors. *How to Garden Indoors & Grow Your Own Food Year Round* covers every aspect of getting off to a great start, from setup, to seed starting, to pests, hydroponics, and more. Take control of your own food destiny and know that even if you don't have a yard or a place to grow, or you simply want to extend your growing season, you can successfully grow your own produce indoors and have a real sense of food security for you, your family, and your community.

Steve and Laura Bartholomew
Directors
Square Foot Gardening Foundation
A 501(c)3 Non-Profit
www.squarefootgardening.org

Preface

A fun question on social media is, "What's your superpower?" I used to answer, "I grow big food from tiny seeds." However, an even greater superpower I have is teaching small-space, high-intensive edible gardening so others can confidently grow at least some of their own food. I've been teaching classes, seminars, and "lunch and learns" at various venues near my home in Maryland since 2010.

When the pandemic hit in early 2020, I was inundated with requests for classes. Because we were soon put under stay-at-home orders, in-person classes weren't an option, so I had to develop a new plan. Thankfully, I quickly pivoted to online classes and consultations and then to on-demand videos.

People were afraid of what the future might hold, and it felt good to empower them by alleviating at least some of that fear and anxiety. It was great to be able to expand my reach from Maryland to as far away as Peru. In a short time, hundreds of students became more secure growing their own nutritious, organic food at their homes and community gardens.

Even before the pandemic, a common theme frequently crept into conversations with potential students, especially those who needed to depend on community or allotment gardens: "I *really* want to start a garden, but I'm afraid someone might steal my food." Sometimes I heard, "My landlord, or Homeowners Association (HOA), won't let me grow food. Can I garden indoors?"

Initially, I recorded three basic gardening classes to teach people various small-space methods and get them up and running quickly. These were followed by more specialty classes on advanced techniques like vertical gardening, growing tomatoes, and fall and winter gardening without a greenhouse, and I planned on adding more periodically. I thought about a class on indoor gardening but hesitated.

Then, around 2017, I volunteered for a faith-based organization and was asked to explore different indoor food-growing methods, since our clients were mainly apartment dwellers with little access to reliable transportation to get to a community garden. The next year, I also started volunteering for a nonprofit that gave gardens to wounded veterans. One of my tasks was to research indoor options for growing fragrant herbs on structures that could be wheeled from room to room in a veterans' assisted living facility in southern Maryland. As a military brat and veteran of the United States Air Force, this mission was near and dear to my heart.

The thought of creating an indoor gardening class was always in the back of my mind. Let's face it; I have been doing and researching indoor gardening for quite a while. The scope of the class kept expanding, and soon the *class* was turning into an entire *course*. Then, out of the blue, I was approached by Fox Chapel Publishing and asked if I'd like to write a book on indoor gardening. Thus, *How to Garden Indoors & Grow Your Own Food Year Round* was born.

I hope that the information in this book will save you time and effort by taking advantage of my years of research, experience, and mistakes!

Kim Roman
Owner
Square Foot Gardening 4 U
"Confidently Grow Your Own Food!"
www.sfg4u.com

Contents

Introduction

Why Indoor Gardening?

You've spent the spring, summer, and early fall outside in your garden, but with late fall's blustery arrival, your plants start dying, and you decide to wrap up for the winter. Perhaps you're part of a community garden (a.k.a. an allotment garden) that closes from October to April. It's, indeed, a sad time. Heavy sigh. You still want access to inexpensive, organic food without the grocery store prices, but what can you do?

The solution is simple. Grow indoors!

Whether you choose indoor gardening as your year-round preference or only use it in the cold months, *How to Garden Indoors & Grow Your Own Food Year Round* shows you how easy it is to grow nutritious food no matter your circumstances. This book is your one-stop shop to learn about simple indoor edible gardening even if you have limited space and resources. My promise is to give you clear, concise instructions on several different methods of indoor growing without a lot of technical jargon so you can choose which method(s) work best for you and your situation. (The exception to this is the section on hydroponic gardening—there's just no escaping technical jargon there!)

For the purposes of writing this book for you, I limited my personal growing space to a small section of my home office, plus the top of a small cabinet in my tiny eat-in kitchen and a few larger plants in a spare bedroom. The office space is a little less than 4' x 9' (1.2 x 2.75m) in floor space, the kitchen tabletop is about 23" x 41" (58.5 x 104cm), and the desk in the spare bedroom is a little less than 2' x 5' (61 x 152.5cm). I present several different growing methods and, when possible, show you commercially available options alongside similar DIY projects for you to construct. This demonstrates that even if you have just a small area in which to grow, you can enjoy an incredible amount of fresh food in less than 43 square feet (4 square meters). And if lack of space is not your main concern, this book is still for you: indoor gardening is scalable to suit your needs.

Finding Your Why

Here's a question for you: *Why* do you want to try indoor food gardening?

It's important to ascertain the answer to this question upfront—don't skip past it by saying to yourself, "Oh, I'm just interested and think it will be fun!" With a clear why, you'll remember your overarching goal or goals, which will keep you motivated when you experience a setback. Once you've come up with your why or whys, you should physically write them down on a piece of paper and tape it to a wall or put it on your refrigerator for motivation.

My why may not match yours, but you might still see parallels. One of my on-demand classes at *www.sfg4u.com* is called Fall and Winter Gardening Without a Greenhouse. I do a good bit of growing outdoors year-round here in Maryland, Zone 7b. If you're farther north, just look at my friend, Niki Jabbour, who grows outdoors all year long without a greenhouse well up into Canada. She even wrote two books on it—*The Year-Round Vegetable Gardener* and *Growing Under Cover*. I love extending my outdoor season, but I have to admit, crop choices are a bit limited. My personal why is expanding the choice of what's available for me to grow during the colder months.

You are limited to cool-weather crops when you're growing outdoors in the fall, winter, and early spring, Your choices for outdoor growing are basically lettuces, greens, and root vegetables. Indoors, when you provide a nice, warm room and supplemental light, you can include many warm-season crops like tomatoes, eggplants, peppers, and tender herbs that wouldn't survive in your outdoor winter garden. Do they grow as big and bountiful as they would outdoors in the summer? Not really. Do they grow as quickly? Not always. But a fresh, homegrown tomato in the dead of winter is always a joyful treat.

Does your why match mine, or do you have a different why? If you're still stuck, here are some common reasons for cultivating an indoor garden, and not just in the cold months:

- You don't have anywhere to garden outdoors.
- You have space outside, but your Homeowners Association (HOA) doesn't allow edible gardening.
- You've gardened in the spring, summer, and fall, and you want to continue to provide your family with nutritious, organic produce in the warmth of your home, even in the worst weather.
- You have an outdoor fall and winter garden but want to expand your choices.
- You've always liked to be prepared "just in case."

If you still haven't found your why or whys, head on over to Chapter 1 for more ideas. Then write them down, like I directed earlier, so that they can motivate you in the lows.

Learn from My Mistakes and from My Friends

My business tagline is "Confidently Grow Your Own Food!", so this is the perfect time for me to tell you what I tell all my garden class students: never get discouraged when gardening. You can do everything one hundred percent perfectly and still have a crop failure. It happens whether you're a brand new gardener or a seasoned expert. You can be disappointed, even pout and stomp your feet a bit, but never give up. Your victories will be entirely worth it. I had a Sun Gold cherry tomato plant that I brought indoors to overwinter. It reliably produced fruit for a full year, much of that time while indoors. The vine grew to a whopping 11 ½' (3.5m) in length! Start small and add to your indoor garden a bit at a time. It will probably become a fun and addictive challenge for you to grow more and more food indoors as the years go by.

Frankly, you can learn a lot from my mistakes and missteps, and let me tell you, there have been quite a few through the years. But taking the time to learn about and choose the right method or methods will save you time and money by not purchasing unnecessary gadgets and containers, buying or making the wrong growing medium, etc. And nothing is worse than a costly error that results in a damaged wall or floor due to water or mold, especially if you rent or lease your space. We'll cover this too.

I also contacted some gardening experts to help me explain things to you at different points in the book. No matter how much research I've done, I always feel better when I can ask someone I trust and who has the knowledge for clarification on sticky points, especially when the information online is conflicting.

So, sit back and relax while I help you "Confidently Grow Your Own Food . . . Indoors!"

PRODUCT AND RESOURCE DISCLAIMER

You'll notice that I've included a few commercially available products throughout the book. These are not endorsements of the products, and they represent just a small sample of what's available on the market. If products have been given to me by the manufacturer to try, I disclose that fact. If something doesn't live up to my expectation, I tell you that too.

The Resource section at the end of the book lists helpful contact information and product sources as of the writing of this book. Of course we all know, things change, people leave, and companies fold, so forgive me if you have trouble contacting a particular organization.

Gallery of Indoor Gardens

There's nothing like seeing someone else's thriving indoor gardening to whet your appetite for your own tasty homemade crops! People around the world, in all kinds of climates, and with all kinds of spaces and budgets love indoor gardening. Here are some personal success stories from individuals and families who have learned and grown with their own indoor food gardens. Get inspired to start work on your own!

Tessa Agrey

Edson, Alberta, Canada | Website: *www.hopeinnovation.ca*
In my garden: tomatoes, peppers, lettuce, kale, beans, basil, strawberries, arugula

There are so many reasons I pursued indoor gardening. For one, I wanted to make sure that I had a food source that I controlled so that no matter what happens, I can eat. For another, fresh produce is so expensive and goes bad so fast. I was wasting hundreds of dollars a month buying food and never eating it because it would go bad before I had the chance to. Now I can simply pick what I need, and the rest continues to grow more leaves and fruits instead of growing mold!

Now that I grow my own veggies, they taste so much better. It feels like I am discovering new foods. My lettuce is no longer bitter and watery, but has flavor. I have never tasted tomatoes that are so juicy and sweet. It's also a true mood booster to have living plants in my home, especially during the long, freezing, snowy months of winter.

In the photos you can see my hydroponic setup with grow lights, the Eden Garden by my company, Hope Innovations. I love this system because it doesn't require seed refill pods, there's no transplanting necessary, and it grows produce super fast—I'm harvesting leafy greens every three weeks!

Lan Huynh

Philadelphia, Pennsylvania | Instagram and YouTube: @Plant4Table
In my garden: lettuce, herbs, peppers, cucumbers, eggplants, cherry tomatoes, peas, strawberries

My indoor garden is completely hydroponic. I use three different systems: AeroGarden, Gardyn, and iHarvest. I live in USDA plant hardiness zone 7, which means I can only grow things outdoors about five months out of the year. I enjoy growing hydroponically indoors because it allows me to garden year-round.

Having a garden indoors is an amazing experience because we always have lettuce, herbs, peppers, and cucumbers available just a couple steps away from the kitchen. Our meal ingredients are always fresh and nutritious! I especially prefer to grow lettuce indoors because it prefers cooler temperatures—it doesn't do well in the summer heat. We stopped wasting store-bought lettuce that we couldn't use up fast enough.

Celie Brayson

Ullesthorpe, Leicestershire, United Kingdom | Instagram: @milestone_cottage
In my garden: dill, parsley, arugula

Coming from the concrete jungle, this was our first attempt at growing anything, inside or out! We wanted to start becoming as self-sufficient as possible, so we used pallet wood, old coffee jars, and a couple of pots found in local charity shops to create this wall herb garden. We also designed the garden to fit aesthetically with our ongoing home renovations.

We absolutely love indoor growing and found it to be a great starting point for us as novices. We planted everyday things that we knew we'd use, such as dill, parsley, and arugula.

Our indoor herb garden, as we usually call it, has given us the confidence boost we needed to carry on growing! We now have a live patio allotment currently on the go, filled with potatoes, carrots, lettuce, and onions. Next stop, full garden allotment!

Andreas Chrysomallis

Amsterdam, The Netherlands | Instagram: @andreas_chrysomallis and @fermentationart
In my garden: various edible flowers, dill, chives, parsley, beets, radishes, carrots

This is an indoor garden that I set up in my apartment in Amsterdam. Due to the pandemic, I had some extra time, so I decided to start the whole process from scratch. I followed an old traditional method—I germinated different kinds of seeds wrapped in wet paper towels. I placed these bags in the sun for 10 to 15 days, and then I began to plant them in the soil.

As a chef, I love to use fresh herbs, edible flowers, and mini vegetables in my dishes, so this was a great opportunity to grow my own and explore indoor gardening. I have a variety of edible flowers; my favorites are violets, nasturtium, and marigolds. In the herb section, I have dill, chives, and parsley, which I also use daily in my home cooking. Lastly, I have a variety of mini vegetables; my favorite are beetroots, radishes, and carrots.

Felicia Feaster

Atlanta, Georgia | Instagram: @fafeaster

In my garden: mini tomatoes, lettuce, beans, peas, habaneros, mint, thyme, oregano, Swiss chard, kale

Though I've done plenty of outdoor gardening, this is the first year I have tried to grow seedlings indoors. Growing an indoor garden and starting plants from seeds is uniquely satisfying and taps into the nurturing side of gardening: you have a front-row seat to the delicacy and magic of seedlings sprouting and growing every day. It feels like my personal little plant nursery where I can nurture these baby plants until I introduce them to the outside world of my deck garden.

My indoor growing setup, situated near a long window in the hallway between my kitchen and my bedroom, is a combination of "hacks" in which I am using two hydroponic growing systems to grow edibles and also sharing their light with other nearby seedlings. I use mason jars and vintage coffee mugs to grow some of the seedlings, as well as special seedling bags in my hydroponic gardens. Because I work for HGTV, aesthetics are important to me, so I do like having some cute plant labels, vintage containers, and ornamentals mixed in to coordinate with my home. Once the seedlings are established, I transplant them to my edible containers on my deck, right outside this window, and begin an often losing battle to keep the squirrels out of them.

I am lucky as a frequent garden writer and editor for HGTV to receive trial plants to test. For example, right now, I am growing PanAmerican Seed Kitchen Mini Tomato Red Velvet, from a series of plants designed to be grown in a sunny windowsill for people without a garden.

Jessica Doyle

Sewell, New Jersey | Website: *www.theoutsidersfarm.com*
In my garden: snowbird peas, various herbs, various mints, kale, spinach, various melons, various tomatoes, June-bearing strawberries, bell peppers, lemons, limes, eggplants, carrots, and more

I work pretty simply. I grow my plants in containers, both store-bought and self-made. In the dark winter months, I grow them under grow lights and in a greenhouse, if necessary. Otherwise, I grow all of my plants in my house with natural light.

I started indoor gardening because it was easier to watch the seedlings and see how each plant grows and reacts to lights, water, and soils throughout the day. My children and I love to watch the plants grow all the way up from seeds and eat the fruits, vegetables, and herbs right from the containers.

I love to grow organic vegetables, fruits, herbs, and melons. My favorites to grow are watermelon, cucumbers, limes, blueberries, and rare types of mints. Some of my special plants include berries and cream mint, ambrosia muskmelon, patio snacker cucumbers, and calamondin (miniature oranges).

Eilidh McKnight

Glasgow, Scotland | Instagram: @the_scottish_garden_allotment
In my garden: tomatoes, chilies, herbs, pea shoots, spring onions, microgreens, mushrooms

I initially started indoor vegetable growing because in Scotland there is such a short outdoor growing season. I decided to start experimenting with indoor growing, and I found it extends the scope of what I can grow here hugely. I have been growing various vegetables and herbs indoors for a few years now. I love the freedom it gives me to grow fresh food that would otherwise be out of season.

Currently I am growing in soil, but I plan to build a hydroponic system with integrated grow lights next. The kit I'm currently using is a small, heated propagator to start tender seeds, with grow lights to supplement light during the winter. In summer, my plants thrive on my kitchen window, which is ideal for cooking. I even built a small shelf across the window to maximize the space!

In this particular setup, I am growing pea shoots and spring onions to be used small (at right), and I also have a couple of tomatoes and chilies under the light (at left). My favorite things to grow are tomatoes, chilies, and herbs; I find that these are comparable in size to houseplants, which makes them very accessible. In the future, I plan to add potted citrus trees and increase the amount and variety of food I grow indoors over winter.

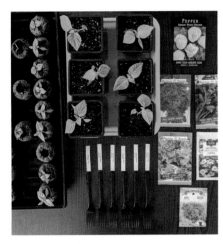

Tatiana Serdyuk

Aurora, Ontario, Canada | Instagram: @mdm.sll

In my garden: microgreens, lettuce, tomatoes, pea shoots, and much more

My husband and I pursued food indoor gardening as a secondary activity to our passion for cut flowers. Where we live, summers are generous but winters are long. Growing microgreens, leafy lettuce, and dwarf tomatoes indoors can be a nice distraction from bad weather.

Early on in our gardening journey, the only space we had was on a small stair landing where I could hang a couple of grow lights and fit two shoe trays to catch water runoff. Today I have more growing space than I ever dreamed of, but I will never stop rooting cuttings on windowsills or setting up salad bars by the kitchen sink, and I still rely on my original full-spectrum grow light from the stair landing.

My secret to success is choosing produce that's ready to harvest within 14–50 days. When choosing seeds, I also look for labels such as "dwarf/miniature," "hybrid," or "suitable for containers." Chances are, those plants have been bred to stay compact or hybridized to be self-pollinating.

Dhanya Venugopal

Bayonne, New Jersey | Instagram and YouTube: @aromas.awake / aromaS awake
In my garden: salad greens, peppers, chilies, tomatoes, onions, zucchini, cabbage, cauliflower, broccoli, beans, green peas, mint, lavender, cilantro, strawberries

As people who love cooking, growing our own vegetables brings us a lot of joy. I also love sharing cooking recipes and garden adventures on my YouTube channel! Since we always live in rented apartments, the only way we can grow plants is to have an indoor garden. And since we move around a lot, we try to keep our costs as low as possible by buying inexpensive stands (from Ikea) and pots (from Dollar Tree).

Our current apartment does not get any direct sunlight, so we use a single Spider Farmer SF-1000 light fixed on a tripod, which we reposition between the plants to get the proper amount of light.

Emily Kichler

Highland Heights, Ohio | Instagram: @thecompost.xyz
In my garden: kale, collard greens, bok choy, basil, celery

I was inspired to start an indoor garden by the mutual aid work going on in my area. I really wanted to grow something fresh that I could bring to a community fridge over the winter, using a minimal and affordable setup and repurposed or thrifted pots. I was interested to see what was possible with a small budget.

I started growing in early 2021, expecting to have some produce for the winter. With two clip lamps and 5000 Kelvin, 800 lumen LED lights, I started from seed a number of kale, collard green, and bok choy plants. I also grew some basil (from seedling) and celery (regrown from a stump). With this setup, I didn't get veggies in time for a winter harvest, but I was able to start harvesting in late spring. With higher-lumen bulbs, longer grow light hours, and/or more clip lamps, I know I could grow the veggies a bit faster next time. Overall, growing veggies is always a humbling learning experience.

Lorna Kring

Sechelt, British Columbia, Canada | Website: *www.gardenerspath.com*
In my garden: basil, green onions, cucumbers, radish sprouts, tomatoes

I have a couple different setups in my home. My countertop grow kit is an economical and easy way to jumpstart cool-weather greens like kale, lettuce, spinach, and Swiss chard or tender, heat-loving annuals like basil, cucumbers, and tomatoes. They are excellent medicine for the garden lover who can't wait for spring.

Sprouts are another great countertop option. All you need is a mason jar and a perforated lid. The result is bright, zesty, and packed with nutrients.

I also like to hold my cucumbers and tomatoes indoors until outdoor overnight temperatures are consistently above 50°F (10°C). I've set mine up on a couple of folding tables next to a west-facing window in the family room. I also have some basil and citrus trees overwintering in a different west-facing window.

PART 1

GETTING STARTED

In this part of the book, we'll discuss several great reasons you'll want to garden indoors. If you read the Introduction and still haven't figured out your why, this chapter will help.

We'll also cover the important planning steps you'll need to take before you even start your garden so you can work smarter, not harder. Ultimately you'll save time, money, effort, and frustration.

Finally, we'll strategize how to more evenly distribute the weight of your containers and prevent damage to your floors, walls, and table. This is a no-disaster zone!

Many of us have likely brought herbs indoors over the winter, but have you ever grown food crops? It's time to start!

CHAPTER 1

Advantages to Gardening Indoors

The biggest advantage of indoor gardening is not having to deal with the weather.

One only needs to do a quick online search to come up with many reasons to grow food indoors. Let's walk through a few of the most common ones here.

Better Weather

Most people complain about the cold, but frankly, the summer heat and humidity affect me even more, and I know many of you readers feel the same. Indoor gardening isn't just for wintertime! With indoor gardening, not only can you save yourself the pain of facing the elements, but you can have a great deal of control over the "weather," i.e., the temperature and light, in your indoor garden.

About the only downside of indoor gardening is that your body won't be producing as much vitamin D as it would if you were outside in the garden absorbing the sunshine. So make sure you're still getting enough safe sun exposure.

Local Eating

Another weather-related factor is the lack of availability of certain foods during the winter months at your local grocery store. Granted, nowadays you're able to find almost anything you want in your local market at any time of the year, but at what cost to your pocketbook and the environment? Your winter tomato has traveled who knows how many thousands of miles to grace your dinner table. I'm an advocate of eating seasonally and purchasing locally, but growing indoors means that in many cases, with proper planning, you'll be able to eat what you like at almost any time of the year.

Fewer Pest and Disease Problems

Indoor gardening doesn't mean that you won't have *any* problems, but there will be fewer kinds of bugs to contend with. For instance, moths won't be hovering over your plants and laying eggs that will become hungry, hungry caterpillars to decimate brassicas like your cabbages and kale. Also, if you set up your indoor garden correctly, your plants shouldn't experience as many disease problems.

Relatedly, while they don't bother your plants, I don't know about you, but I get eaten alive by mosquitos in the summer months. For me, that is the biggest deterrent to gardening at any time of the year, so I'm grateful not to have to battle them.

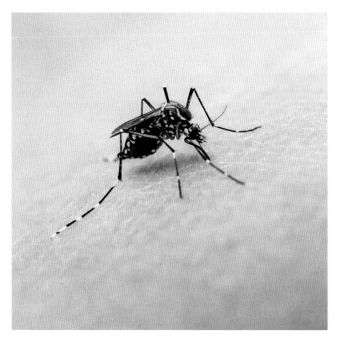

An advantage to growing indoors is not having to deal with pests like mosquitos.

You also won't have to contend with deer, birds, squirrels and other critters stealing your harvest just as something yummy ripens. The benefits just keep rolling in!

Money Savings

You'll save money by gardening indoors. . . eventually. Start-up costs will put a dent in your budget initially, but if you factor those costs over the life of the hydroponic kit or other growing apparatus, you'll soon find that you're saving money over what you'd pay at the grocery store or farmer's market for fresh, organic produce. This is especially true if you learn how to start your own plants from seeds rather than buying transplants—see Chapter 12 for more about seed starting.

Food Safety

You'll know exactly what's in/on your food and can use organic methods if that's important to you. For instance, did you know that the apples you buy in the grocery store might be as much as ten months old? Not only have they been sprayed with pesticides, but also with coating chemicals to extend their lifespan. Other produce is sprayed with fungicides. Even if the produce you buy has been pre-washed at one point in time, think of how many hands and machines have touched it since then. Was the machinery properly cleaned? Did the workers handle things in a safe manner? When unbagged produce is misted at the store to keep it fresh, do you know when the water hoses and emitters were last sanitized? Growing your own food means that you have complete control over the entire process.

Fun for the Kids

How many children really know and understand where food comes from? Indoor gardening is a great way to spend quality time with your children and grandchildren while integrating different school subjects and life lessons.

Once, my then five-year-old grandson was asked to draw food in his pre-kindergarten class. He did nothing more than color the piece of paper brown. The teacher thought he hadn't understood the assignment and said, "Reece, you're supposed to draw *food*." He said, "I *did*! I drew the soil in my Oma's garden. There are seeds underneath that will make food."

Adaptability and Accessibility

If you or a loved one is older or has a medical condition that makes it hard to venture outside, indoor gardening is a great way to keep active in comfortable, climate-controlled surroundings. You'll be able to grow your crops at the right height without bending over or reaching up too high.

In fact, during the writing of this book, I experienced a health scare due to a side effect of a new medication. Extreme fatigue meant I wasn't able to keep up with my outdoor garden. However, I was still able to produce a good amount of food in my indoor garden without physical exertion.

Empowerment

Finally, you'll feel extremely strong by pushing the envelope. Nothing is more empowering than feeding your secret rebellious streak as well as your stomach by defying Mother Nature, especially during the winter months, by growing your own food.

The customizable aspect of indoor gardening will also allow you to tailor your work to your needs and give you a sense of personalization that will connect you even more with your work. While my garden teaching career has been based on small-space, high-intensive methods, which are presented in this book, you can scale these methods up or down based on your desires and your available space to create just the garden for you.

Children love the wonders of the garden, and you can teach them a lot while getting them involved.

THE AIR QUALITY MYTH

Why didn't I mention in this chapter that growing an indoor garden would improve the air quality in your home and provide additional oxygen? You've probably heard that plants purify the air of volatile organic compounds (VOCs) and provide the room they're in with fresh oxygen. I really hate to burst your bubble, but that's just not true. In 2019, the Journal of Exposure Science Environmental Epidemiology debunked this myth when they analyzed twelve different studies on the subject spanning thirty years.

Modern ventilation systems mean we never have to worry about oxygen production and removal of VOCs in our indoor air. In order to make an appreciable difference in air quality, you would need at least ten plants for every square foot (0.03 square meter) of room space.

When plants were put into a chamber and VOCs were pumped in, something would happen, and the VOCs would, indeed, decay over time. The scientists assumed it was the plants, but it turned out to be the microbes in the soil that actually did the work. The review concluded that ventilation would remove VOCs much faster than plants or soil microbes ever could. Grow plants indoors for their beauty and the food they provide, but don't rely on them to clean the air.

There are plenty of great reasons besides the air quality myth to grow plants indoors.

CHAPTER 2

Before You Start

No matter how you garden, always start small and expand over time.

Motivational speaker and self-development author Brian Tracy says it best: "Every minute you spend in planning saves ten minutes in execution; this gives you a one thousand percent Return on Energy!" I don't know about his math skills, but I agree that you can save a tremendous amount of time and effort by focusing on planning rather than implementation.

There are many things to think about before you even plant your first vegetable. Read through each of the questions in this chapter to come up with the outline of a plan that will work for your needs.

What Should You Budget For?

Figure out how much money you intend to allocate to start your indoor garden, and stick to your budget as much as possible. Remember, you can expand your garden little by little over time to spread out the costs. Don't overbuy, start too big, become frustrated, and then abandon what should have been fun and empowering and which became simply a money sink.

First, understand the basic components of an indoor garden to get an idea of starting costs. At its most basic, indoor gardening requires a pot, soil, plants/seeds, and

Can't afford a large indoor garden? Start with simple DIY projects (like this one, featured on page 168), then save up for things you want to add, like grow lights, self-watering containers, etc.

fertilizer. These can range from free (such as a recycled pot) to averages of $10 (for seeds), $15 (for a bag of soil), and $10 (for fertilizer). So you could get started for as little as $35. **(See an example of this budget on page 28.)**

When you go beyond the basics to an intermediate level, you will start adding things like grow lights (typically $17–$25 apiece), specialized testing tools for hydroponic systems (typically $10-$25 apiece), larger bags of soil, and furniture or structures to plant on ($35 and up). These can raise total starting costs to $100 or $150, which is still achievable for many budgets. **(See several examples of these budgets on page 28.)**

Don't be afraid of DIY solutions, either. Up-front costs of larger indoor gardens will be significant if you need to rely completely on commercially available products, but costs will be lower if you are able to recreate some of these systems through the do-it-yourself projects in this book. I'll show you how to make a small self-watering (wicking) planter out of a 1-gallon (3.8L) water bottle and some cheap materials. Compare this virtually free planter to one sold in the store for around $20. If you have some basic tools like a drill with a hole-cutting bit, there are hundreds of online videos showing how to build a hydroponic system for at least half the cost of a commercially available kit. As another example, I have used a Garden Tower 2 that boasts room for fifty plants (pictured on page 52); it costs nearly $400, but you could mimic this setup by buying a stackable planter with space for nine plants, a bag of good soil, fertilizer, and a few packets of seeds for less than $150. Just add a sunny window, and you'll be able to keep yourself in salad greens and herbs for several years.

Beyond the start-up costs, you'll need to consider the cost of additional water and electricity to dedicate to your plants over time. For most beginner indoor gardeners, water costs will be negligible, though constant. The average American shower uses 2 gallons (7.6L) of water per minute, and you'll likely use 1 gallon (3.8L) of water or less per week for a small indoor setup, so you can see how adding watering to your water bill is unlikely to cause a noticeable increase. If you're able to use natural lighting, your electricity costs will be free. If you can't open the windows, the cost of running a fan a few hours a day is again minimal.

Once you've purchased everything, factor the cost of these materials over the number of years you can reasonably expect them to last. For instance, good containers will probably last a decade or more. You may be able to repurpose items from around the house or from a secondhand store. (Be sure to read the section on safe plastics on page 71 before reusing found objects.) Even though containers are usually a one-time purchase, you'll continually need to buy the consumables. For example, you will need to add fertilizer and supplements to your growing medium (or hydroponic system) every few weeks. If you purchase a lower-quality bagged growing medium, that soil will need to be completely replaced every year or two. This season, you might not have any pest or disease problems, but next season you might get hit hard and need to make or buy fungicides or pesticides. You need to be ready for these costs over time. In an average year, in an average-size indoor garden, the cost of thwarting pests and diseases, if you run across a problem, will be about $20. Fertilizer and supplements might be an additional $40 or less per year.

SAMPLE STARTING BUDGETS AND COSTS

$50 Super-Basic Beginner Setup

With these materials, you'll be able to grow shallow-rooted veggies and herbs that don't require a lot of light, such as leaf lettuces, baby greens, beets, radishes, peas, and beans. Herbs you can grow include cilantro, mint, oregano, parsley, tarragon, and thyme. In general, plants that need less light tend to have shallower root systems. This first sample budget, since it doesn't include supplemental lights, is ideal for shallow-rooted veggies. However, if the pots you choose are deep, you can grow deeper plants; just know that deeper pots tend to cost more.

Six 6" (15cm) round plastic pots with saucers $11	Balanced 8-8-8 dry fertilizer $10
8-quart (8.8L) bag of organic soil for vegetables...............$16	Seeds for shallow-rooted veggies/herbs..........................$13

$50–$70 Microgreen or Sprout Setup

Microgreens and sprouts are most efficiently grown in dedicated setups that can be purchased all-in-one.

Microgreen or sprout growing kit (all-inclusive)........ $50–$70

$100 Large Soil System with Lights

Because we're adding some inexpensive grow light strips that include the red spectrum, you'll be able to grow things that require more light, including a couple short-season or dwarf varieties of tomatoes and peppers.

Six 6" (15cm) round plastic pots with saucers $11	Balanced 8-8-8 dry fertilizer $10
Six 8" (20cm) round plastic pots with saucers..................$25	Red/blue 20W LED grow light strips $17
1 cubic foot (0.03 cubic meter) bag of soil for vegetables..$20	Vegetable and herb seeds $17

$100 Deep Water Culture Hydroponic System

If you're interested in a starter hydroponic system, you could try this approach without too much investment.

Hydroponic float/raft kit....................................$35	Up/down pH adjuster...$16
Liquid kelp fertilizer concentrate......................................$17	Extra pH test strips..$8
TDS/EC/temperature meter $12	Seeds..$12

$150 Large Vertical Soil System with Lights

When using a shoe tower, explained in Chapter 7, you'll be able to save floor space by growing things on a vertical structure. However, the plants will have to be short varieties to fit on the "shelves." It's perfect if you have tall windows or a glass door where you can place the tower.

Six 6" (15cm) round plastic pots with saucers $11

Six 8" (20cm) round plastic pots with saucers.................$25

1 cubic foot (0.03 cubic meter) bag of soil for vegetables..$20

Balanced 8-8-8 dry fertilizer $10

2 red/blue 20W LED grow light strips $34

Shoe tower...$35

Vegetable and herb seeds $15

$150 Nutrient Film Technique Hydroponic System

With an NFT hydroponic system, you'll need to grow crops that all have the same nutrient requirements. See Chapter 8 for more information.

NFT hydroponic kit $85

Liquid kelp fertilizer concentrate....................................$17

TDS/EC/temperature meter $12

Up/down pH adjuster..$16

Extra pH test strips...$8

Seeds..$12

EVEN MORE MONEY-SAVING TIPS

- Go to a discount or dollar store for your planters. Check the recycle number to make sure they are safe (see Chapter 7 for information on safe plastics). If the drainage holes aren't sufficient, you can enlarge them or make more of them with a drill.

- Make one of the DIY planting containers discussed in Chapter 13 from safe recycled plastic bottles and jugs.

- If your upcycled container is deeper than you need it to be, fill the bottom with things like unsalted peanut hulls, aluminum foil balls, used Styrofoam blocks, etc., and only fill the top 6"–8" (15–20cm) with soil.

- Share seeds with your friends. Have each of you buy three packs of seeds and swap the extras. Discount stores also sell seeds in the spring. They're not going to be organic and heirloom seeds, but that's fine. You could also attend a seed swap (see page 162).

- Instead of an indoor garden tool kit (usually $20), use a recycled plastic fork, spoon, and knife along with a small pair of scissors.

- If you don't have a suitable watering can (usually $15), use 20-oz. (590mL) soda bottles, drill small holes in the cap, and fill with water. The size of the holes will determine how gently the water will flow. Five or more 1/16" (0.2cm) holes are perfect for a fine spray for newly seeded areas, while a single 1/4" (0.6cm) hole will create a stream of water for a more established plant.

- Consider offsetting your increased electrical or water costs by directly decreasing your usage in other ways. For example, take shorter showers, turn off the tap when your brush your teeth, and unplug appliances and turn off power strips when they're not in use. All these tips and more can help save resources in any household, but you may benefit from knowing you're directly making space in your home for the new resources you're using for your plants.

What Are Your Yield Goals?

Even if cost isn't of concern, I suggest everyone start small when learning how to garden indoors. This is especially true if you're new to gardening in general. A small tabletop plug-and-play hydroponic system for some lettuces or a few containers of herbs to begin with will help you ease into the process. The goal for your first year should be to learn *how* to garden indoors, not to completely feed a family of four.

Your indoor garden can be very small or scaled up depending on the space that's available to you. However, just because you have a large house or a large area to grow, doesn't mean you shouldn't think about exactly what you want to accomplish. Why plant too much if all you really want is to provide a fresh salad every couple days? Just how much of your food do you actually want to grow? Be realistic. If you've never gardened before, do you even know how many heads of lettuce you'd need for your family, and how to use the strategy of succession planting so that you

have a fresh harvest each week? Feeling a bit anxious? Take a slow, deep breath, and I'll help you with this in Chapter 10.

We've already discussed how budget may affect your plant options, and later in this chapter, we'll discuss how lighting may affect your options as well. Keeping this in mind, think about what you'd like to grow in your indoor food garden. Maybe you already have a long list of veggies written out, but are they practical for growing indoors? Check the details of your "dream veggies" in Chapter 11 to make sure they are realistic for your first foray into indoor gardening.

How Much Time Do You Have?

Realistically, think about how much time you will be able to devote to your garden. Initially, you'll spend a significant amount of time planning, learning, purchasing materials, constructing or setting up your system(s), etc. Eventually, depending on how large your garden is, you'll likely spend an average of ten minutes per day to water, tend, and harvest

Your crop choice may be determined by the method of growing you choose. These greens and lettuces will be great grown either hydroponically or in a soil-based system.

your crops. Luckily, this is typically an amount of time that anyone can afford to spend. Again, taking the time to plan correctly will result in fewer mistakes and less wasted time by not having to undo something and start over.

Do You Own or Rent?

Yes, this is an important consideration. Of course, if you own your home, you'll want to minimize the possibility of damage and the expense that would come from having to replace flooring or remediate mold. However, one thing my mother taught me that I'm going to pass along to you is the philosophy of treating someone else's things even better than you would your own. I encourage you to be a thoughtful tenant and take extra precautions to prevent

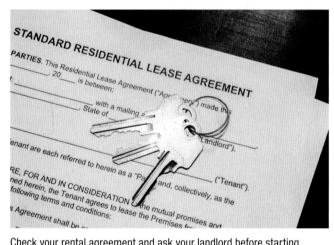

Check your rental agreement and ask your landlord before starting your project.

Initially this window seemed too sunny for lettuces that like a part-shade environment, but these translucent blinds can be lowered to provide a little shade as needed.

any damage to your landlord's property. After all, you'll be liable for repairing the damage. We'll discuss prevention of potentially costly damage in Chapter 3; you may want to choose a specific type of system or start small depending on your housing scenario.

What Sites Are Available to You?

You know your space and know what will be completely off-limits, but I encourage you to look around your entire home to find surprisingly viable locations for your indoor gardening activities. Realize that you don't have to grow everything in one location in your house. For example, I've carved out a small area in my south-facing office where I also use supplemental lights to do the bulk of my growing. However, I also grow some herbs in a sunny south-facing window in my kitchen without any supplemental lighting, and I've placed a few plants that need a cooler location upstairs in a spare bedroom with a west-facing window. In that spare room, I also do the video recordings for my classes, using a video ring light and a floor lamp for supplemental lighting. The ring light produces 5500 Kelvin—and you'll find out the importance of that number to plants in Chapter 6.

Be creative when identifying suitable locations for your garden. Can you use a grow tent with supplemental lighting and good air exchange down in your basement? Absolutely! How about using an "over-the-toilet" shelf to raise your plants to window height in any room? Great idea. Is it possible to safely waterproof and modify an old bookcase into a lush garden? Yes!

You might see a tiny office/living room in this photo, but I see a huge sunny window with a windowsill and a lot of horizontal surface on that window-height cabinet that would be great for an indoor garden.

Check the light coming in from the window several times a day to assess how much total light you'll get.

What's Your Home's Lighting Like?

If you don't want to use supplemental lighting, a critical consideration will be providing sufficient natural sunlight for your plants to grow well. Different crops have different light requirements in order to thrive and produce food. Before we discuss that in more detail, though, you need to know how much natural light is available for you to even work with.

First, ascertain your home's cardinal direction, a.k.a. its orientation or position relative to the sun. The sun rises toward the east and sets toward the west, of course, but its precise position depends on the time of year and your latitude. Use a compass application on your smartphone.

Once you know your home's orientation, look around your house and identify which windows get the most sun. Those will be the ones that face south in the northern hemisphere and face north in the southern hemisphere. Note how many hours a day a plant would receive light in front of these windows. Check frequently during the day, and watch how the sunlight travels throughout the room from morning until evening.

The time of year in which you're growing is important too. Understand that the sun's angle will change throughout the year, and that you'll receive far less light from the same window from late fall until early spring, so you may need to change what you intend to grow during different seasons if you don't want to use supplemental lighting. If you're growing a crop that needs a lot of light, such as tomatoes, during the winter months, even a south-facing window will not be enough—you'll need supplemental lighting.

Also, look outside. Anything that causes less light to penetrate into the room will affect how well plants will grow. If you're assessing the sunlight during the winter months, for example, and there's a deciduous tree outside, think about how much shadier it will be in the room when there's a full canopy of leaves in the spring and summer. Clean windows mean more light too.

Now that you've thoroughly assessed your available natural lighting, it's time to put it into practice. First, research the conditions favorable to each of the crops you are interested in growing. Divide your growing list into three categories: full sun, part sun, and part shade. Here's the difference:

- Full sun (outdoor) = 6+ hours of direct/bright sun per day
- Part sun (outdoor) = 4–6 hours of direct/bright sun, which may include afternoon sun
- Part shade (outdoor) = 4–6 hours of moderate sun, with protection from hot afternoon sun

These numbers are a good starting point, but they're not the end of the story. When growing indoors, you'll need to compensate for not having a lot of constant direct/bright sun as compared to growing outdoors. In the spring and summer, most plants will need about 1.5 times more than the amount of light than your research tells you they need, because these references will be for crops grown outdoors rather than indoors. In the late fall and throughout the winter, you'll want to double the hours of light because of the lack of sunshine at that time of year. So, a more realistic indoor gardening light list would be:

- Full sun (indoor) = 9+ hours of direct/bright sun per day in summer; 12+ hours in winter
- Part sun (indoor) = 6–9 hours of direct/bright sun, which may include afternoon sun, in summer; 8–12 hours in winter
- Part shade (indoor) = 6–9 hours of moderate sun, with protection from hot afternoon sun, in summer; 8–12 hours in winter

For example, lettuces, greens, and some herbs only require about 4 hours of direct/bright sun when grown outdoors. That means, if you're growing them at the window in spring or summer, they'll need about 6 hours. In late fall through winter, they'll need about 8 hours. Without any supplemental lighting, you might have enough light to grow these crops in an east or west-facing window during the summer, but they'll do best in a south-facing window from late fall to early spring.

If you want to grow fruiting crops like tomatoes, peppers, cucumbers, eggplants, blueberries, etc., there's just no way around it—you'll need supplemental lighting. Even though the lights look quite bright, your plants will require up to 16 hours of supplemental lighting in late fall and winter to grow and produce fruits. You might be able to grow them in a sunny window during the summer, but be ready to supplement their lighting if they don't look like they're doing well. Also, if you are in an apartment surrounded by other buildings all around, without any natural light, you will have to depend on supplemental lighting.

For a more in-depth discussion on natural and artificial lighting, see Chapter 4.

How Much Weight Can You Handle?

No, no, I'm not asking about your lifting skills—another major consideration is the weight of everything you need to grow your plants. And I mean *everything*. Can your floors handle all the extra weight? If not, you may have to stick with a small hydroponic system rather than a large soil-based growing method, or spread out your growing space over a larger area, or take some of the weight off your floors by using a wall system or growing on a window sill.

First, let's consider the weight of soil. If you're thinking of using soil you've gathered from your yard, which I *do*

Soil and water weigh a lot, and it adds up quickly as you add more plants to your garden.

Adding materials like vermiculite or perlite will help lighten a heavy soil-based growing system, which can be really valuable when you're using a large setup like this one.

A hydroponic system like this weighs considerably less than a soil-based container system.

not recommend, the typical outdoor soil is about 35–50 lbs. (11.3–22.6kg) per cubic foot (0.03 cubic meter), even if it's bone dry. Besides lacking the nutrients needed, yard soil is usually quite a bit heavier than a growing medium specifically made for indoor growing. If you use a good indoor growing medium, it will be about 13–20 lbs. (5.9–9kg) per cubic foot (0.03 cubic meter). As you see, you can dramatically cut down the weight of your indoor garden simply by using the appropriate growing medium. Another way to decrease the weight of your garden is to use a particularly lightweight growing medium. Check out the sidebar in Chapter 6 for some great indoor soil recipes from my friends at Veteran Compost.

Another factor is your choice of materials for your containers. If your containers are deeper than your plant

roots need, put in a couple inches (about 5cm) of a super lightweight material on the bottom of the container before adding your soil. See Chapter 7 for more ideas to lighten the load.

After soil, the next weight concern is water, which comes in at around 8.3 lbs. per gallon (4kg per 4 liters). One way to help with this is to vary your watering schedule so that all the soil is not saturated at the same time. Another strategy is to use a lightweight mulch on top of the soil to help slow evaporation.

My lightweight, 36-plant hydroponic system uses only about 3 gallons (11.5L) of water. So for the 40" x 20" footprint (102 x 51cm), that's not too bad, coming in at less than 30 lbs. (13.6kg). In contrast, my Garden Tower 2 soil-based system sits atop a 30" x 30" (76 x 76cm) homemade storage cube with heavy-duty casters. Between the cube, everything that's stored in it, the tower, 7 cubic feet (0.2 cubic meters) of lightweight indoor soil, and 3 gallons (11L) of water, it adds up to about 250 lbs. (113.5kg). The footprints of both systems are pretty close, but the weight difference is tremendous:

Hydroponic system: 5.55 square feet (0.52 square meters) = 30 lbs. (13.6kg)

Garden Tower + storage: 6.25 square feet (0.58 square meters) = 250 lbs. (113.5kg)

I'm fortunate that my house is located on a concrete slab, so this isn't a factor in my site assessment. For more information on how to distribute heavy weight on your floors, see Chapter 3.

Do You Need to Lose Weight?

Again, I'm not being personal, but there are ways to lighten the load with your soil-based methods. If you're growing shallow-rooted veggies, you can add vermiculite or perlite to the bottom few inches (about 5cm) of deeper containers. You can also mix a little extra vermiculite in with your growing medium if it's too heavy.

I buy bulk unsalted peanuts in the shell. When I'm done eating them, I save the shells and put them in the bottom couple inches (about 5cm) of my containers to take up some of the volume in a container with very little weight. Make sure they are unsalted, as salt can kill your plants. Because they are an organic material, they will eventually deteriorate, which is fine.

Another option is expanded clay balls used in hydroponics, which are lightweight. They won't deteriorate like peanut hulls, and they are a good option because they will fill a lot of space with very little weight. They will also help if you've overwatered the soil. Because of their round shape, I've occasionally experienced one of them getting lodged in a drainage hole, preventing excess water from escaping, so periodically check to make sure the holes are not clogged.

What Method(s) Will You Use?

After you've assessed your space, you're ready to determine what growing method or methods you'll use. There are so many methods from which to choose and many variations within each method. For instance, let's look at container gardening. You can grow plants in large pots on the floor. However, if floor space is at a premium, or you want to limit the amount of weight on your floors, narrow boxes

Take your time when considering what method or methods of growing you'll use. While vining tomatoes can be grown using some hydroponic methods, this dwarf variety is happy to grow in a container.

on windowsills, wall gardens, or hanging planters would be good solutions. Maybe a hydroponic setup is more to your liking, but do you know which setup would be best for the crops you want to grow? If you've never gardened before, growing microgreens or sprouts are two easy first methods to try. While they're both easy to grow, there are so many different ways to grow them, which we'll cover in Chapter 9. For instance, you can grow sprouts in something as simple as an old jar, or use a multi-layer system called a sprout tower to grow several varieties at the same time. For microgreens, you'll use trays, but you need to choose if you want to grow them using water (hydroponically) and some sort of mat or sprinkle the seeds on top of a special soil.

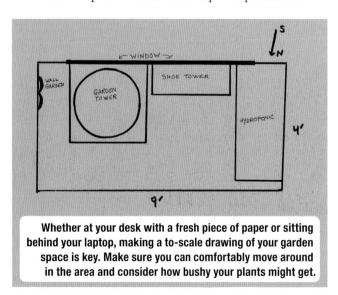

Whether at your desk with a fresh piece of paper or sitting behind your laptop, making a to-scale drawing of your garden space is key. Make sure you can comfortably move around in the area and consider how bushy your plants might get.

CHAPTER 3

Site Preparation

The more time you take with site preparation, including using protective materials like this, the less likely you'll be to experience damage to your house.

There are several steps you may need to take to prepare your home or room for your indoor garden before you ever bring the actual soil, plants, and pots to live with you. Let's walk through them together.

Floor Weight Distribution

In the last chapter, you learned how to determine the approximate weight of your potential garden. How you prepare your floors to handle that weight is determined by several factors.

If your house doesn't have a basement, in many regions, it's likely built on a concrete slab. If this is the case, it means you won't have to worry about the weight of your garden as long as you're placing it on the flooring directly on top of the concrete (as opposed to on an upper level).

If you have a basement below your house rather than a concrete slab, examine the structural integrity of the flooring from below and make sure you aren't exceeding the weight limit with your garden.

If your house has a basement or is elevated off the ground, or you live in an apartment complex or want to place a garden on an upper floor, you will need to think about distributing the extra weight so the floor can handle the load. This is particularly true when using a large, heavy, freestanding, soil-based system.

Let's take a look at a typical floor to get an idea of what we're dealing with. First there are the floor joists, which are individual lengths of lumber running parallel to each other 16" (40.5cm) apart on center (following the United States standard, at least). Next, ¾" (19mm) plywood is laid over the joists crossways and attached to the joists. Then your actual flooring, what you're stepping on, is on top of that. This flooring could be carpet, laminate, vinyl, tile, hardwood, etc.

Most local building codes rely on the International Residential Code, which requires floors in non-sleeping rooms to support a minimum live load of 40 lbs. (18kg) per square foot (0.1 square meter). Sleeping rooms must be able to carry 30 lbs. (13.6kg).

In my example given in the last chapter, my Garden Tower 2 weighs about 250 lbs. (113kg) and covers an area of 7 square feet (0.65 square meters). That comes to 35.7 lbs. (16.2kg) per square foot (0.1 square meter). That's fine for a non-sleeping area, but not if I'm putting it in my upstairs bedroom. And the weight goes up if I'm standing in that area.

If you are going to exceed the weight limit of your floor, your options depend on whether or not you own the home and have the ability to make structural changes and additions.

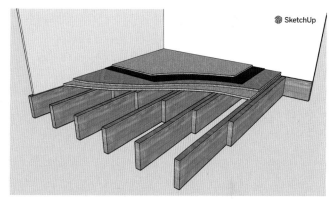

Here's what the typical floor system looks like—joists, plywood, and flooring (in this case, gray carpet). If your indoor garden is too heavy for your existing floors, you can easily distribute the weight by adding a vapor barrier and another sheet of plywood (the top two layers shown here).

If you own your home and have access to the floor joists from below (i.e., you are growing on the ground floor and have an unfinished basement below that area), you can strengthen the floor by sistering or connecting another joist to each existing joist before laying the subfloor. You could also simply install additional floor joists evenly spaced between the existing ones. These approaches also work great if you're planning to convert an unfinished attic to use as your growing space.

If you don't own the home or are in an apartment, your goal should be to distribute the weight between several floor joists. As you see from the image above, there's already a layer of plywood subfloor that sits on top of the floor joists to distribute the weight. Then your flooring (i.e., carpeting, hardwood, tile, etc.) is placed on top of this subfloor. If your floor feels "bouncy" or "squishy," the subfloor might not be sufficient to carry the extra weight of your indoor garden. In this case, I recommend adding a thin foam vapor barrier/underlayment and an additional sheet of ½" (9mm) or, better yet, ¾" (12mm) plywood on top of the existing flooring to distribute the weight even more. Plywood typically comes in a 4' x 8' (240 x 120cm) sheet. If the area you're covering isn't that big, ask the lumber yard or home improvement store to cut it to your specifications. A vapor barrier is meant to help prevent damage from humidity, but it will not protect the flooring from a large amount of water. See the section at right for more info on that.

When in doubt whether or not your floors can handle the weight of your indoor garden, hire a structural engineer to assess the situation for you and make recommendations.

Hanging on Walls

Just like floors, your wall is typically made up of lengths of lumber spaced equally apart at 16" (40.6cm) on center. Instead of being called joists, these are called studs. They are typically covered by sheets of drywall. If you have an older home, your walls might be made of lathing and plaster, brick, or stone. Check your lease agreement for information about hanging heavy items on the wall if you rent your place.

There are too many variables regarding hanging wall fixtures to cover in this book, so you'll need to research the proper techniques for hanging heavy objects such as a wall garden on your particular type of wall. Some options to consider, depending on how your walls are constructed, will be wall anchors, a French cleat, or metal Z-clips. If you are at all hesitant, hire a professional to figure it out for you, execute the installation, or both.

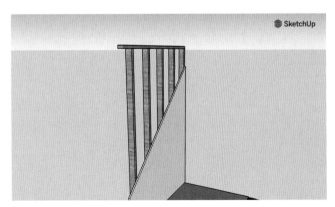

Here's what the typical stud and drywall wall looks like. When possible, the studs are where you should be screwing in heavy fixtures.

Protecting Floors, Walls, and Tables

In addition to ensuring your floors and walls can handle any extra weight you're planning to throw at them, you'll want to protect them from scratches and water damage. My existing floors are laminate, so I chose to use an absorbent rug with a rubber backing. This would also help protect hardwood flooring. The rubber backing is so the rug doesn't slide across the floor, not to stop water, so having a wet vac on hand in case of spills is recommended. Carpeting can be protected from soil and a little water by using a protectant spray and some plastic sheeting. Tile floors don't need as much protection from water, but they would benefit from a thin foam underlayment to prevent scratching.

The only time you are likely to have a truly catastrophic water incident is if you're using a hydroponic system. Make sure the joints are tight. Most systems work well with just friction fitting the pipes and joints together. If you want added security, though, you can glue them—but note, if you glue PVC together, it is permanent! See the sidebar in Chapter 7 for the safe use of PVC and glue. For extra security, consider adding some kind of catch basin (see the sidebar on page 39).

I use an absorbent, rubber-backed rug to minimize potential damage to my laminate floors.

Using corrugated plastic or even an inexpensive plastic shower curtain can keep your walls from getting wet.

A felt-lined plastic tablecloth protects a table from both water damage and scratches.

 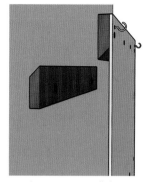

This wall hanging system models one way to ensure no wall damage. The French cleat holds a lot of weight and additional strips of wood hold the system away from the wall to prevent moisture buildup. The yellow panel is rigid plastic to prevent water damage.

When using any method where you're hanging something on the wall, in addition to ensuring you hang it properly with regard to its weight, be sure to provide a moisture barrier as well as adequate air circulation to prevent mold and protect from damage caused by water.

For my cloth wall pocket (a type of vertical growing system that hangs on a wall), because the product I was using was not made specifically for an indoor application, I chose to use a French cleat to hang it (which is a heavy-load-bearing hanging method), added strips of wood to hold the system away from the wall for air circulation, and added a moisture barrier to prevent water from reaching the wall. When using any wall system, be sure not to overwater and to immediately wipe away any overspray. If you use a commercially available wall system, the manufacturer should provide materials and instructions on how to prevent wall damage.

Finally, tabletops and countertops are easily protected by using a flannel-backed, waterproof plastic tablecloth or even a waterproof shower curtain.

WATER DAMAGE

Remember I promised to warn you about things that happened to me to keep you from making the same mistakes I did? When hooking up my hydroponic kit for the first time, I didn't properly secure the flexible tubing that runs from the small plastic bin on the floor that holds the nutrient/water solution to the uppermost PVC pipe. I got a minor drip, but over time, it could have done some real damage. While I was repairing that, I accidentally bumped into the fitting that allowed the water to drain back into the bin. You guessed it: all the water drained out and my laminate floor was drenched. Thankfully, I caught it in time to pull up the rug and dry it before mold had a chance to form and before the laminate was ruined.

For the second go-round, I used a hairdryer to warm the tubing so that it fit more snugly over the nipple, which stopped the drip. I now have a series of aluminum chafing pans under the whole hydroponic setup that together hold more water than the entire volume in the hydroponic unit. Better safe (and a little ugly) than sorry!

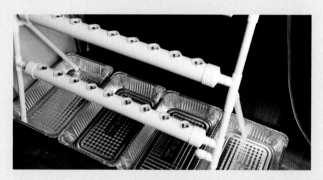

These aluminum chafing pans will prevent water damage should I have a leak in my hydroponic system.

WHAT PLANTS NEED

PART 2

In this part of the book, we'll talk about the six basic things that food crops need: light, air, soil, water, nutrients, and warmth. With some hydroponic systems, plants will use a substrate instead of soil, which will be covered in Chapter 6.

- Light: Natural sunlight, or supplemental lighting, helps with photosynthesis so plants can produce their food, the starch/sugar they need to survive.
- Air: Carbon dioxide in the air also helps with photosynthesis, and the air space in soil provides water with a place to collect and gives roots room to grow. When discussing air in Chapter 5, we'll focus more on the benefits of air circulation and ventilation.

- Soil: Soil is not the same thing as dirt. Dirt is dead; soil is alive. Most plants need a good, fertile soil teeming with beneficial microbes, organic matter, and nutrients for healthy growth.
- Water: Think of water like the blood in our circulatory system. The plant root hairs absorb water from the soil, it travels throughout the plant, and eventually it is transpired out through the stems and leaves.
- Warmth: The proper temperature helps plants maintain optimal growth. Some like it hot, while others prefer the cool.

With few exceptions, plants need the same things: light, air, soil, water, nutrients, and warmth.

CHAPTER 4

Light

The proper type and amount of light makes all the difference in turning a tiny sprout into a flourishing, food-producing plant.

Natural sunlight and/or supplemental lighting are critical for photosynthesis, which is the process by which a plant creates its food. If you don't provide enough light, your plants will starve and eventually die. If plants don't receive the proper type of light, they may not bear fruit at all. You may have heard the term "leggy" before; this refers to when plants get tall and skinny and develop fewer leaves. This results when plants are too far away from the light source and have to stretch their stems to search for more light.

Different plants require different amounts and types of light. For instance, you'll read that tomatoes need pretty strong light for at least 6–8 hours a day, while lettuces can get by on less direct light for about 4 hours per day. But those figures are for when they're grown outdoors. You'll need to double that figure when growing indoors. If you don't intend to use supplemental lighting, your crop selection will be limited to those plants and herbs that only require about 4 hours of light per day. You can also expect your crops to grow at a slower rate than if they are grown outdoors or under strong supplemental lighting.

When planning your garden, you'll want to research how much light each crop requires and if it needs to be direct or indirect light. This information should be readily available on the seed packet or plant tag. If you're growing food in a couple different areas of your home, group plants with similar light requirements together whenever possible.

Whether using natural or supplemental lighting, it's a good practice to give each plant container a quarter or half turn if possible so that the plant gets a good amount of light all over it. This can be done as frequently as you'd like, but it should be done at least once a week.

Natural Sunlight

Be ready with gauzy curtain panels in case your window is too sunny or hot.

If there's not enough natural sunlight available for your plants to grow, you'll need to use supplemental lighting, which we'll cover in more detail later in this chapter. Conversely, sometimes you'll need to protect your plants from too much sun during the hot months. In this case, be ready with inexpensive, gauzy netting fabric to diffuse the harsh summer sun even if the ambient air temperature is pleasant. If the sun streaming into the room increases the temperature, you'll also want to increase airflow—see Chapter 5.

Whether natural sunlight or supplemental, light is crucial for the photosynthesis that allows plants to create their food.

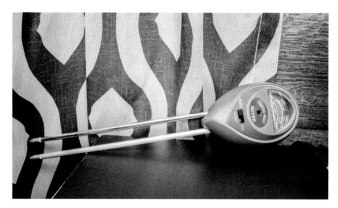

A 3-in-1 meter allows you to check light, pH, and moisture with the flip of a switch.

A light meter is handy to check for the brightness of either the sun or grow lights. I use a 3-in-1 meter that measures light, pH, and moisture. To get an accurate reading, put the meter as close to the plant as possible and point it toward the light source.

Planning for the Sun

Choosing a room with a south-facing window is best for those living above the equator in the northern hemisphere; a north-facing window is best for those in the southern hemisphere. Some plants like morning light, and for others, afternoon sun is best. Just because the sun looks good at a specific moment in time, don't be fooled. Pop in the room a few times a day and snap a photo. You'll notice the sun moving across the room. Keep track of how many total hours of sunlight you are getting. Read more about day length at right.

Pay attention to how the angle of the light penetrating the room changes during the seasons. The sun will be closer to the horizon during the winter months and higher in the summer.

Understand that the path of the sun will be different depending on the season. In the winter, the sun is lower in the sky and is present for fewer hours of the day. In the summer, the sun is higher and will be out for more hours—but, because it's at a higher angle, the sunbeam might not travel as far into the room. It's complicated, but once you start paying attention to the path of the sun around your house, it will make sense.

To allow the maximum amount of light to reach your plants, keep your windows clean, both inside and out.

Day Length

While some plants *can* grow with lighting 24 hours a day, most need a period of darkness in order to bloom and produce fruits. This is called photoperiodism. According to Brittanica.com, photoperiodism is "the functional or behavioral response of an organism to changes of duration in daily, seasonal, or yearly cycles of light and darkness. Photoperiodic reactions can be reasonably predicted, but temperature, nutrition, and other environmental factors also modify an organism's response."

I know what you're thinking—"Kim, you told us you weren't going to confuse us with a lot of technical mumbo jumbo and jargon." You're right—so let me interpret. Basically, some crops won't produce well, or at all, if they're not given enough light, while others won't produce if they're given too much light.

I can't think of any indoor gardening plants that grow optimally with 24 hours of continuous light, so if you're

The amount of light in an average day in a given season will affect how well your plants grow—or potentially prevent some of them from growing properly!

using supplemental lighting, don't keep it on all day and all night thinking you're going to get a better or faster harvest. As much as plants need light for photosynthesis, they also must have that certain period of darkness in order for their metabolism to work properly. Remember, photosynthesis is how plants create food. It's not healthy for us to eat continuously 24 hours a day, and it's the same for plants.

A plant that requires a long period of darkness is termed a short-day (or long-night) plant. Short-day plants form flowers only when the day length is less than about 12 hours. As you would imagine, these are usually the plants that flower, produce fruits, and then seed in the spring and fall, when days are shorter and nights are longer. If these plants are exposed to more than 12 hours of light per day, bloom formation does not occur.

Other plants require a short night to flower. These are termed long-day (or short-night) plants, and they only bloom when they receive more than 12 hours of light, like we experience during our summer months.

To confuse matters even more, some plants form flowers regardless of day length. Botanists call these day-neutral plants. Tomatoes, corn, cucumbers, and some varieties of strawberries are day-neutral.

Keep all of this in mind when you're figuring out how long to keep your supplemental lights on.

Supplemental Lighting

The topic of supplemental lighting can be confusing, so take your time in this section. Even after you read this chapter and have a preliminary idea of what you want, do more research online to fine-tune your decision. Be aware: the more you read, the more you'll receive conflicting information.

If your goal is just to start seeds indoors, and you only want to take the plants to the seedling or transplant stage for growing outdoors, you can simply buy the right fluorescent tubes or LED bulbs and the corresponding light fixtures at your local hardware store for a fraction of the price of what are commonly marketed as "grow lights." However, if you plan to grow plants for food entirely indoors, which this book assumes you are, you'll likely need to invest in something more specialized.

You may have read that if the main parts of the plant that is eaten are the leaves (e.g., lettuces and herbs) or roots (e.g., carrots and radishes), you'll need lights that emit blue light, which helps make chlorophyll, whereas if the plants you're growing produce flowers and you eat the fruits (e.g., tomatoes and peppers), then you'll need red lights to encourage blooming. But that's not the full story—plants actually benefit from the addition of a bit of yellow and green light too.

I like to use a fixture with a combination of mostly full-spectrum bulbs to cover the need for yellow and green light

These vertical lights are great for a Garden Tower.

A red/blue spectrum light includes the red spectrum for fruiting crops and the blue spectrum for good leaf growth. It doesn't appear as bright to the human eye, and it will make your plants look a ghastly shade of grayish purple, but they will love it.

Take your time and do your research when choosing the right lightbulb for your plants' needs. Full-spectrum LEDs, like these, are a great multi-purpose choice and come in a variety of styles to fit your growing space.

with the addition of a few extra red and blue bulbs. Please note that when just using red and blue lights together, without the addition of white light, your plants and the surrounding area will look a horrible shade of purple.

Types of Lightbulbs

Let's look at the different types of supplemental lightbulbs and tubes that you might purchase.

Incandescent and **halogen** lights produce a lot of heat and are not a good option. They'll make the room too hot and can scorch your plants if they're placed too close.

Fluorescent tubes and **compact fluorescent lights** (CFLs) are much more energy-efficient than incandescent lights and produce a brighter and whiter light. CFLs have the traditional design that allows them to be screwed into a normal lamp or light fixture, while the tubes have pins that are used in specific light fixtures. These bulbs come in cool (bluish), warm (orangey/reddish), and full-spectrum. Because the light is weak, you'll want them about 2"–3" (5–7.6cm) from your plants in most cases.

Light-emitting diode (LED) lights offer stronger, cooler lighting and are quite energy efficient. You can find them in full-spectrum, individual color, and multicolor lights. Since LEDs are stronger, place them ideally 12" (30cm) away from plants.

There is another, less common lighting option out there called **high-intensity discharge** HID lights. They are extremely bright and even more efficient than fluorescent lights. There are two different kinds: metal halide (MH) and high-pressure sodium (HPS). MH lights are great for seed starting or leafing and root plants, and HPS lights are for flowering and fruiting plants. Both types of HID lights need different, specialized fixtures. You'll want to do more in-depth research if you're interested in using HID lights, but most readers won't need to venture there.

No matter which type of lightbulbs or tubes you use, keeping them clean will help them emit as much light as possible. With the lights turned off and the fixture unplugged, use a feather duster or soft, dry cloth to gently clean the bulbs.

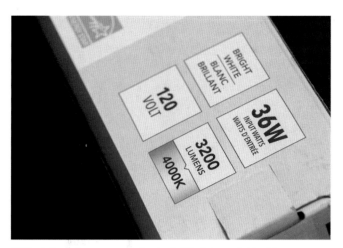

All the information you need about a lightbulb is available right on the package.

This 6,400-Kelvin tube light has enough red in it to grow fruiting crops, but you know it's full-spectrum because the tube itself is white.

Measuring Light

Lightbulbs display values on the packages and bulbs themselves stating how much light they emit. Here's a quick tour through what these measurements mean.

Watts

You've probably seen watts listed on the package of your old household incandescent bulbs. Watts are the measurement of power consumption. Wattage is important to your wallet when you pay your electric bill. Basically, by knowing the wattage, you can figure out how much it will cost you to run the light. However, the wattage isn't directly related to the quality of the light as it relates to helping your plants grow.

Lumens

Lumens, from the Latin word for light, describes the brightness of the bulb. The higher or lower the number on the package is, the brighter or dimmer the light will be. You might also see this listed on the package as "light output." It's a little deceiving, because lumens only measure how bright a light looks to the human eye.

The ideal brightness range for growing seedlings is 2,500–5,000 lumens, although 2,000 will do in a pinch. The lumen value is really only helpful when you're starting seedlings and need bright, white light. Red or blue lights don't look as bright to the human eye, so when you're using just a red light or a blue light, they'll seem quite dim.

Kelvin

Kelvin describes the color temperature—that is, warmth or coolness—of your lights. It's important to know the Kelvin of your lights in order to choose the proper ones for growing.

The red/orange side of the spectrum is considered a warm color temperature, while the blue end represents a cool color temperature. As noted earlier, blue light is needed for vegetative growth, so if you're focused on that, you should look for a Kelvin range of 5,000–7,000 K. Red light is necessary to promote flowering and fruit production, so if you're focused on that, you should look for a range of 3,500–4,500 K. For most new indoor gardeners, though, full-spectrum bulbs are usually the way to go. Full-spectrum bulbs mean that the light covers the full color spectrum from red to blue. The advantage to these is that they have all the colors, including green light, which will make plants look more natural to the human eye. Some plants perform even better with full-spectrum light, so these are a good choice.

PAR and PPFD

While watts, lumens, and Kelvin are all useful things to know, when you're talking specifically about grow lights, there's a newer, better way manufacturers let you know how beneficial a light is to a plant: PAR and PPFD.

Simply put, Photosynthetic Action Radiation (PAR) measures the effectiveness of a grow light for plant photosynthesis, which needs a wavelength range of 400–700 nanometers. PAR values are measured in

My favorite full-spectrum light comes from Maxsisun. It's dimmable and comes with a remote control.

For instance, if you're growing on a countertop, there are small tabletop lights that may have one or multiple arms so you can direct the light above each individual pot. Many plug-and-play hydroponic kits (which you'll learn about in Chapter 8) use dedicated lights as part of the system. There are also parabolic lights that clip to the edge of a counter or table; these are commonly used in workshops and reflect a lot of light onto a specific area.

Panel lights can be hung horizontally above your plants on a frame, and some of them can also be used vertically. They can either be larger fluorescent shop lights or LED panel lights.

If you're thinking about HID lights, you'll often see them as a boxy light fixture either hung above the plants or on a tripod.

Now let's talk about grow lights, which are products specifically designed and marketed for indoor gardening. When I contacted the company Maxsisun to get information about grow lights in general, full disclosure: they offered to send me one of their newest models to try. I asked for the smallest unit, which is their MF1000, because I wanted to show someone with a really small space what was possible. At the time of writing, this fixture retailed on Amazon for a reasonable $129.99.

I was stunned by how much light the fixture put out, since it only measures a little over 13.5" x 11" (34 x 28cm). Setup was super simple. Best of all, it came with two different hanging kits and a remote control so that I don't have to fumble around for the switch or jimmy the plugs out of the light socket every time I want to turn the lights off. The remote also controls the intensity of the light from 10%–100%. Several lights can be daisy-chained together and can be controlled by a single remote.

I've had two fluorescent and two small red/blue LED lights for about a decade now, and while they've served me well, neither came with instructions. I was surprised to find out from the MF1000 instructions that when you first start using any grow lights, you should include a 3–5 day acclimation period with the lights at a lower intensity so that the plants can become used to the light. The instructions included a schedule telling me for each plant stage (acclimation, seedlings, vegetative, or flowering) how far away the plants should be from the light, at what brightness the lights should be, and for how long the lights should be on each day. For instance, for the seedling stage, the plants should be 20"–24" (51–61cm) away from the light, and

Photosynthetic Photon Flux Density (PPFD). PPFD, also called PFD, measures the amount of PAR light that hits the plant each second. We don't need to get into the technical details here—you simply need to know that when researching grow lights, look for a PAR value greater than 500μMol/m²/s (micromoles per meter squared per second).

Fixtures

Now that you understand a bit about what type of light your plants need and what types of bulbs are available, let's talk about light fixtures. Pick a fixture based on not only what you're growing, but also where you're growing it.

the lights should be at 60% brightness for 18 hours on and turned off for 6 hours.

After running the MF1000 for a few hours, I tentatively touched the metal reflector hood and then the bulbs, and they were just slightly warm, so I knew it wasn't generating too much heat for the plants. I added a timer to the system myself to make it even more convenient, since I sleep longer than the 6 hours that are recommended as the dark period for some of the growing stages.

Timers are handy when using any grow lights, and I highly recommend their use so that your lights come on and turn off automatically at specific times. Timers come in a wide range of styles and are generally simple to set up and use. One convenient type is the kind that you simply plug into the wall before plugging your lights in through the timer.

In Chapter 2, when you were doing your site assessment, I asked you to make sure that there was sufficient electric power in your room to run everything you need to grow your plants—lights, fans, water pumps, etc. There are a couple ways you can handle this. If you live in an older home without great power, hire an electrician to come in and increase the amperage (amps). Another way to handle this is to get more efficient grow lights with a low power draw of, say, 140W, or look for solar-powered grow lights. If you intend to grow a lot of your food indoors and will use several grow lights, investing in whole-house solar panels to lower your total electrical bill might be a good option. In many areas, you can get solar panels at no cost and buy your electricity from the company for a reduced rate. Using an automatic timer, or turning off the grow lights when the sun is bright, can also help lower costs.

A simple timer plugged into the wall outlet will automatically turn your grow lights on and off.

So, how long should you keep your grow lights on? Besides following any potential manufacturer's instructions that come with a product, you can follow some general rules. If your plant requires 6–8 hours of sunlight when grown outdoors (e.g., crops such as tomatoes, peppers, and eggplants), they should be under lights for 12–16 hours indoors. Those plants that require less light outdoors, such as lettuce, only need about 8 hours of supplemental lighting per day. Group your plants together by light needs if possible to minimize variation and hassle.

CHAPTER 5

Air

Adding even a simple fan to an indoor gardening setup can make a big difference to the health and productivity of your plants.

Air is a critical component for plants to survive and thrive, but they don't just need it above ground. Air must be present in the soil for roots to breathe and grow. Also, if air space is not available at the root level, excess water could cause the roots to drown and rot. This is why both fluffy soil and proper drainage are so important. Those small air spaces, or pores, between soil particles also provide the roots room to grow and are where the beneficial soil organisms live. This topic will be covered in more detail in Chapter 6; in this chapter, we'll focus exclusively on the air in the, well, air.

Aboveground air, and in particular circulating air, is equally as important to a plant's health as air in the soil. Plants need air for photosynthesis and to breathe. As you may have learned in science class, photosynthesis is the process whereby the plant creates food, in the form of a simple sugar called glucose, by using the carbon dioxide from the air, along with water and sunlight.

Although static, unmoving air can be used by the plant for photosynthesis and breathing, good airflow mimics the outdoor environment and is necessary for many reasons: it dissipates outgassing from the plants, prevents excess heat from building up in the room, lessens potential disease and pest problems, decreases odors that come from inevitable rotting plant material, and helps evaporate excess humidity. We'll cover each of these topics in more detail in the following pages. One other benefit of good airflow is specific to young seedlings: blowing gentle air on young seedlings and transplants for several minutes each day simulates the wind they'd encounter outside, which helps them develop stronger stems, resulting in a much healthier plant.

Putting an oscillating fan near your young plants can help them grow stronger as it simulates an outdoor breeze.

Creating Good Air Circulation

My husband and I lived in Germany a total of six years, three years each in Stuttgart and Berlin. A common practice of homeowners throughout the country, and written into many rental agreements, is what's called impact ventilation, or *Stosslüften*. This involves fully opening at least one window for a minimum of five minutes each morning and evening for air circulation. An even more aggressive practice is *Querlüften*, or cross-ventilation, where almost all the windows in the house or apartment are opened, allowing stale air to flow out and fresh air to come in. These practices are done no matter how cold or warm it is outside because German society in general feels that it's that important to health. We could all learn a thing or two from the Germans.

Ventilation can be as simple and inexpensive as opening a few windows a couple of times each day. If it's too humid outdoors and this causes a moisture level problem, you'll need to use other methods.

Opening a window for a few minutes can improve the air quality in your growing room.

One option I use is an inexpensive window fan. If it's pleasant outside, I position the fan so that it pulls the outdoor air into the room for a while. If the outdoor temperature is too hot and humid, I turn the fan around so that it blows the room air outdoors. Even though my window fan has a bug net, once I turn it off, if the outside temperature is too hot or cold, I remove it and shut the window.

Another option is to use a couple of oscillating fans pointed in different directions and angles, which you can switch during the day. A ceiling fan is also a good option—you can switch its direction to draw air toward the ceiling or push warmer air downward to help warm the room a bit in the colder weather.

Opening your air conditioning registers can also help. The disadvantage of using your air conditioning is that it's constantly pointed toward the same area. Just make sure

your cool-loving crops are closest to the A/C vent. One advantage of air conditioning is that it will remove moisture from the air more efficiently than a fan will.

Sometimes I have opened the door to my office, where I do the bulk of my growing, and been hit by a wall of heat, even during the cold season. Small spaces, closed windows, and supplemental lighting can result in a large rise in temperature. That's great for some plants, like tomatoes, eggplants, and peppers, but not necessarily appreciated by your cool-weather crops like peas and greens. When planning your indoor gardening, you might want to identify the warmer areas of your house and, if it's practical, divide your crops accordingly, grouping your cool-weather and warm-weather crops in different areas.

Fixing Bad Odors

One of the most critical reasons to maintain good air circulation is to prevent your growing area from smelling unpleasant. Odors can be caused by a number of things. Plants naturally have odors that might be unpleasant, especially when the leaves start to fade and decay through their normal life cycle. Fertilizers and growing media can also produce unpleasant odors. Any of these odors can get into the soft surfaces of your growing room, like curtains,

A window fan like this one can be used to pull in fresh air from outside or push stale air out of the room.

Don't delay cutting off dying parts of a plant.

carpet, or upholstery, and can waft through your entire home without proper ventilation.

Most of the time, the solution is simply good air circulation, as described in the previous section. Identifying and correcting the problem may take a little time. Taking proactive steps before there's an odor problem is best, but addressing it right away is the next best option. Just like a pest or disease problem, it won't go away by itself, and it certainly will not get better with age.

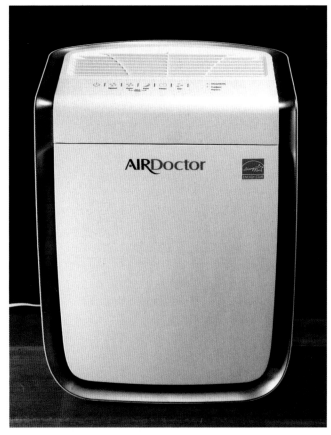

An air purifier can help control odors.

Preventive maintenance is simple: cut any diseased or dying vegetation immediately. It's a good practice to carry a small cup of isopropyl alcohol or other disinfectant and dip your pruners or scissors in the liquid between each plant to avoid the spread of disease. Be sure to remove all diseased, dying, or damaged material from the room as soon as possible. This includes any leaves that have naturally fallen into the containers or onto the floor. Diseased leaves should be thrown in the trash, but non-diseased vegetation can be put into the compost bin, if that is something you

are doing (see more about indoor composting in Chapter 13). Immediately clean, disinfect, and dry your pruners or scissors thoroughly after cutting vegetation, even if none of the plants show any signs of disease. Not only will pruning your plants help prevent odors, but it should also help keep pest and disease problems at bay (see Chapter 14 for more info on this).

If preventative maintenance doesn't successfully prevent a problem and you end up noticing odors, it's time to go from container to container and take a good sniff to see if you can locate the source of the smell. When you come across a foul odor, think of possible causes. Has anything changed? Has your fertilizer gone bad? Did you change to a new type or brand of fertilizer? Did you dilute it enough? If you're growing hydroponically, is the water reservoir clean? Has the season changed and now you're experiencing more humidity than usual? Is more sun coming in the windows, making it too hot in the room? Do you need to change your supplemental lighting to an option that doesn't produce as much heat? Is there enough air circulating in the room?

If you have concluded that your problem is poor air circulation, try an oscillating fan or air conditioning. If that doesn't do the job, the next step is to invest in a dehumidifier (read more about this under Controlling Humidity, below). Another option instead of a dehumidifier is an inline fan and carbon filter. Find a ventilation and odor control kit that best suits your space. The most expensive option to solve the problem is an air purifier, which will remove most airborne particles such as dust, mold spores, pollen, smoke, bacteria, and viruses, which in turn will improve the air quality and thus combat odors. You can run it a couple hours a day and increase the runtime if necessary.

Controlling Humidity

Excess humidity can cause the buildup of bacteria, mildew, and mold, which can not only be harmful to your plants, but can also result in damage to your walls, floors, and soft surfaces. Bacteria and mold can also negatively affect your own personal health. In hydroponic systems specifically, the extra warmth of grow lights coupled with the added moisture of the system can increase the rate of mold and bacterial growth.

It's not as simple as just keeping the air desert-dry, though: too little humidity will make certain plants very unhappy. If the air is extremely dry, it could even pull

MOLD VERSUS MILDEW

Did you know that both mold and mildew are fungal growths? So what's the difference? Technically, mildew is a type of mold. But, practically, the differences come down to two things—what surfaces they grow on and their appearance.

Mold comes in a variety of colors and appears mainly on structures like the insides of walls or appliances and on food. It's usually thicker than mildew, and it usually penetrates the surface of whatever it has started to grow on.

Mildew is most often found on damp paper, fabrics, and plants. It is usually lighter in color, such as light gray or white, and it affects the surface of whatever it's growing on without penetrating very deeply. In gardening, you will often hear of powdery mildew on certain types of plants—definitely something you don't want.

What they have in common is that both problems are usually caused by lack of light, excess moisture, and not enough airflow. Proper ventilation is critical for preventing and resolving problems.

An inexpensive solution to prevent mildew on plants is to use 1 part 2% milk (non-fat milk doesn't work as well) with 4 parts of water mixed in a spray bottle. Saturate the leaves every other week as a preventative, or weekly at the first sign of mildew. There are also pre-made organic fungicide sprays available.

Check frequently for mold inside your appliances, since it loves a warm, moist environment. Prevention is key. Change filters per manufacturer directions, and wipe down any damp surfaces daily. Empty water collection bins on a dehumidifier, or change the water in the humidifier tank every other day. Wipe the bin or tank and any reachable parts of the interior and exterior of the appliance using a soft cloth or paper towel saturated with white vinegar each time you do this.

Darkness, moisture, and bad airflow can create mold and mildew problems. Here's an example of powdery mildew on a leaf.

Because of moisture, appliances like humidifiers, dehumidifiers, and air conditioning units can harbor mold if not regularly cleaned.

moisture out of the soil, which means your plants will suffer, and you'll need to water more frequently.

If high humidity is your problem, an electric fan may help evaporate some of the excess moisture, but it won't remove it. Your air conditioning system will help even more by removing excess moisture, but it still may not be able to keep up with the added moisture of a hydroponic system. If you're using a fan or your air conditioning and find that your room is still too damp, or if you start seeing signs of a moisture-caused disease, consider using a dehumidifier. Depending on the type of dehumidifier you use, you'll need to directly vent it outside or empty a reservoir and change filters regularly. Otherwise, the appliance will be subject to the very mold and bacterial growth that you're counting on it to prevent.

When cold weather hits and you turn on your heating system, your air will tend to dry out. This is the time of year when you notice your skin getting drier, the season in which you walk across a carpeted room and then shock yourself by touching a doorknob. Just like the dry season affects you, it also affects your plants. Dry air can also be a year-round problem for those living in regions with low humidity.

Plants lose, or transpire, moisture through their leaves. The most common sign of too little humidity in your plants is that the delicate edges of the leaves will look dry, feel a little crispy, and eventually turn brown. Of course, this can also happen if you're not watering enough, so check that first.

If you're using a hydroponic system, it will probably put enough moisture into the air. If not, there are things you can do to increase the humidity, like misting the leaves every morning with water from a spray bottle. Watch out for overspray on nearby walls and curtains to prevent damage to these surfaces. This mist will only last a few hours before it evaporates, but that's good, because you want your plants to be dry in the evening when the temperatures drop anyway to prevent fungal diseases on susceptible plants.

You could also use a humidifier. If the room is large, you'll need a large system, or a couple smaller ones, to cover the area. If you're growing in a small space, a tabletop humidifier will work quite well. I've even used my essential oil diffuser and a cool-mist vaporizer. With many humidifiers, you can control how much moisture is released, and some even have timers.

Whether you're adjusting a room's moisture using a dehumidifier or a humidifier, follow the manufacturer's instructions for proper cleaning and always change the filters as directed.

CHAPTER 6

Soil, Water, Nutrients, and Warmth

These seedlings are getting a good start in this moist, airy, nutritious soil.

Besides light and air, soil, water, nutrients, and warmth are the other four essential things that plants need. Because these things are often interconnected, we'll discuss all of them in this single chapter.

Soil, a.k.a. Growing Media

Soil, or any growing medium that does not contain soil, offers plants a number of things. (To simplify, from now on we're going to use the term "soil" even if we're talking about a soilless growing medium.) First, it provides small particles that serve as a structure to hold plants upright and give the roots something to grasp onto. When using many hydroponic systems, that structure is not provided by soil, but by a substrate such as clay balls, cones made of peat moss, or even squishy foam cubes that have slits in them where you place the seeds. These serve a similar structural function that soil does.

Good soil also provides nutrients and contains a fair amount of organic matter. When water is added, these nutrients are absorbed by the root hairs and circulated through the plant. However, organic matter, like compost, is the heaviest component in a good soil. With indoor gardening, we'll depend a bit more on fertilizers.

There are different types of soil for different applications. For instance, a cactus has very different needs than a tomato when it comes to soil structure and nutrients. Check out the sidebar later in this chapter for a couple of great soil recipes from my friends at Veteran Compost. They're great for indoor gardening; there is one for those plants that need a lot of nutrients and one for those that need less.

Don't Use Yard Dirt

So, where should you get your soil? Digging the dirt from your yard, in general, is not a good idea. Put simply, dirt is dead, and soil is alive. Up to one billion beneficial bacteria, along with fungal filaments, protozoa, nematodes, and more, can be found in just a teaspoon (1 gram) of good soil. So, a good soil is teeming with life. What's in your yard is

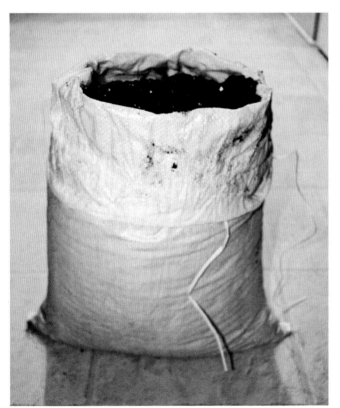

Investing in a good growing medium, whether store-bought or homemade like this soil, will result in healthier plants and a better harvest.

Yard soil usually contains very little organic matter and is not a good choice for growing food.

likely dirt that is devoid of any nutrients that plants need to grow healthy.

If your house is new construction, fill dirt has likely been used to level or elevate the ground. This dirt is a mix of various things like clay, rock, sand, and subsoil. Below that can be tons of construction waste. The thing that fill dirt is lacking is what plants need to grow well: good organic material.

But don't think that you're out of the woods if you live in a house that's been around for decades. The Environmental Protection Agency (EPA) warns that, "Soil, yards, and playgrounds can become contaminated when exterior lead-based paint from houses or buildings flakes or peels and gets into the soil. Soil may also be contaminated from past use of leaded gasoline in cars, from industrial sources, or even from contaminated sites, including former lead smelters. Lead is also naturally occurring, and it can be found in high concentrations in some areas." You may be blessed to live on old farm property with great-looking soil, but you have no idea what chemicals may have found their way into it.

If you must use your yard soil, get a comprehensive soil test first. Tests can be purchased online, or you can check with a local nursery or garden center to see if testing is available. In this case, make sure they are testing for both contaminants and nutrients. You'll gather samples from several areas and mail them to a lab. Once you've had the soil tested and everything's safe, you'll want to mix in other ingredients to make the soil lighter, as what's in your yard is certainly heavier than commercially available soils specifically made for indoor growing. In addition to identifying any contaminants, a soil test will also let you know what nutrients your soil is deficient in so that you can add those before planting.

Commercial Bagged Soils

A solid choice for a beginner indoor gardener is to use commercially available, lightweight bagged soils suitable for indoor use. Contact a local compost or landscape company and explain to them that you are specifically looking for a clean, lightweight soil for indoor use. Some may be willing to custom blend a soil for you.

There are many good brands available for purchase online, too, but one of my favorites is from a company called PittMoss®. Instead of using peat moss, which is a common bagged soil ingredient, PittMoss is a combination

There are several options for commercial bagged soils. One of my favorites is PittMoss, which uses waste paper instead of peat moss.

of recycled paper and organic additives. It provides excellent aeration, good drainage, has a near-neutral pH, and requires about two-thirds less water than an average soil. Plus, a 2 cubic foot (0.06 cubic meter) bag weighs less than 17 pounds (7.7kg), which is super lightweight. I've used it in the wall pocket garden featured later in the book specifically for these reasons.

Homemade Growing Media

If you're making your own lightweight growing medium, you'll use ingredients like compost and vermiculite along with some other things like peat moss and fertilizer additives.

If you'd like to take more control over your soil ingredients, making your own growing medium is a great option. Although the common term for the

HOW MUCH SOIL WILL YOU NEED?

This can be a little tricky. Smaller bags of soil are sold in quarts, while larger bags are sold in cubic feet. If you have several different sizes and shapes of pots, I suggest using a conversion calculator website. My favorite is *www.volumecalculators.com*. This chart will help you translate container sizes for standard-size round and square pots and give you a rough approximation of how much soil you'll need.

Pot Size (inches)	Soil Needed (quarts/gallons)	Soil Needed (cubic feet)
ROUND POTS		
6"	1 qt / 0.25 gal	0.03 ft³
8"	4 qt / 1 gal	0.13 ft³
10"	12 qt / 3 gal	0.40 ft³
12"	20 qt / 5 gal	0.66 ft³
16"	40 qt / 10 gal	1.33 ft³
18"	60 qt / 15 gal	2.00 ft³
SQUARE POTS		
12"	11 qt / 2¾ gal	0.48 ft³
15"	23 qt / 5¾ gal	0.89 ft³
RECTANGULAR POTS		
Use an online calculator such as *www.volumecalculators.com*		

substrate you're growing in is "soil," it's actually best to make what is more correctly called a soilless growing medium. Outdoor soil and dirt are quite heavy, are usually lacking in nutrients, and are not good for indoor applications. In general, your homemade growing medium will contain combinations of the following:

- Light and airy materials like peat moss or coco coir
- Lightweight water-holding materials like vermiculite or perlite
- Nutritious organic matter like a mix of compost and worm castings
- Mineral additives like lime, calcium, greensand, and potassium
- Animal byproducts like bone meal, blood meal, fish emulsion and meal, and composted manure
- Plant byproducts like plant meals, kelp, seaweed, or wood ash

Depending on what you're growing, your formula will be different, but the largest percentage should be the first two ingredients, approximately 35% by volume of peat and/or coco coir, 35% vermiculite and/or perlite. Add to this about 15–25% compost, and the remaining 5–10% should be a good combination of several different mineral additives, along with animal and plant byproducts. I've included a couple of recipes from Veteran Compost in the sidebar on the next page, but you can look online for more indoor soil recipes.

It's best to mix up a small batch and see how it works before going whole hog—another reason to start small with your indoor gardening. Perhaps start with a commercial growing medium while you test your own recipes for a season or two. Then get an analysis of your growing medium to see if there are any major deficiencies, adjusting as suggested by the report. Some testing universities/companies don't test soilless media, so ask first before purchasing a testing kit.

Of course, if you're using some hydroponic systems, you might not use soil at all. In that case, you'll use some type of substrate that will support plant roots, along with nutrient-filled water. We'll cover the different types of hydroponic systems in Chapter 8.

RECIPES FOR HOMEMADE GROWING MEDIA

Here are two great recipes from Julie Laudick Dougherty, who has a Master of Science degree in Agroecology from Ohio State University; she is the soil scientist at Veteran Compost in Aberdeen, Maryland.

Since I'm an Air Force veteran, I was thrilled to learn of Veteran Compost, which is located about an hour from my home. They have served my clients and me well since 2011, providing compost, vermicompost, soils, and advice. I've watched Justen Garrity, an Army veteran and the owner of Veteran Compost, go from a small compost pile and a truck to now running two good-sized operations with several employees and a fleet of vehicles. A third facility is in the works.

Each recipe below is for approximately 1 cubic foot (0.03 cubic meter) of medium, so you can scale it up as needed. As a point of reference, there are 30 quarts (28.5L) in 1 cubic foot (0.03 cubic meter). For an easy measuring scoop, the typical 32-ounce (1L) yogurt container is 1 quart. Measurements don't have to be precise, though, so don't stress.

Container Mix

This recipe is ideal for established plants. You can increase the blood meal and bone meal to ½ cup (120mL) each if your compost isn't as nutrient-rich.

- 14 quarts (13L) coco coir (a.k.a coco fiber or coir)
- 8 quarts (7.6L) compost
- 4 quarts (3.75L) peat moss
- 4 quarts (3.75L) coarse vermiculite*
- ¼ cup (60mL) blood meal (for nitrogen)
- ¼ cup (60mL) bone meal (for phosphorus)

Seed Starter

This recipe is ideal for starting new plants from seeds. It's also great for microgreens and herbs grown in containers, since they don't need a ton of nutrition. As a matter of fact, using a very rich growing medium for microgreens and seed starting will hinder germination, resulting in a smaller crop. If you are doing a denser seeding of baby greens and you don't mind slightly lower germination rates, you can use the container mix, or a 50/50 mix of seed starter and container mix.

- 18 quarts (18L) coco coir (a.k.a coco fiber or coir)
- 4 quarts (3.75L) compost
- 4 quarts (3.75L) peat moss
- 4 quarts (3.75L) coarse vermiculite*
- ¼ cup (60mL) blood meal (for nitrogen)
- ¼ cup (60mL) bone meal (for phosphorus)

Optional Ingredients (for both mixes)

- 2 tablespoons (15g) sulfate of potash (for potassium)
- 2 tablespoons (15g) azomite (for trace minerals)
- 2 tablespoons (15g) mycorrhizal inoculant (to help your plants take in the nutrients and protect them from pathogens)
- Kelp meal (for nitrogen, phosphorus, and potassium)

*Vermiculite is ground mica that is heated until it expands. It is then put into a hopper with successively smaller and smaller mesh screens. What is left on the top is extra coarse, which is a little too chunky for making your growing medium. Coarse vermiculite is what you'll want to look for. Medium will do in a pinch, but fine or extra-fine is not at all suitable. You may have heard that vermiculite contains asbestos, but that's a myth. Because of the persistent rumor, it is thoroughly tested, so agricultural vermiculite is perfectly safe to use. If you can't find it locally, it's available online at places like Greenhouse Megastore, Uline, and Amazon.

You'll want to use different media for different purposes.

Tap water can be used for your plants depending on its quality and whether you filter it.

Water

If you're hooked up to city/municipal water, you may want to filter it before using it to water your plants. This is not usually necessary if your house is on well water. The reason there's a problem with city water is because of the chlorine that can harm delicate plant leaves and potentially kill some of the soil's beneficial microbes. It really depends how much chlorine your city uses; it's not a huge problem in many places, but if you smell a strong odor of chlorine (think of the smell of bleach), you'll want to take steps to reduce the amount of chlorine in your water. Be aware that you don't want to remove *all* of the chlorine, because small amounts are needed by the plant for proper growth.

What can you do to reduce the amount of chlorine in your water? First, put your water into a jug or watering can and let it sit for about 24–48 hours so that a little of the chlorine dissipates. The second thing to do is to water just the soil without drenching the leaves. Both of these strategies also help your plants because they prefer a room-temperature bath to a cold shower. Of course, there are exceptions—if the air is inhospitably dry, you should mist your plant leaves regularly.

When using a hydroponic system or when growing microgreens, you should also be concerned about the water's pH level. On a scale of 0 to 14, pH describes how acidic or basic (alkaline) your water is. A pH below 7 is acidic, a pH of 7 is neutral, and a pH above 7 is basic. Unfortunately, I can't tell you what the ideal level is for plants as different plants like different environments.

HYDROGELS

The jury is still out on whether hydrogels are helpful or harmful. There's no doubt they can be beautiful on decorative plants, though.

Hydrogels, water marbles, gel beads, moisture crystals, water expandable polymer beads—no matter what you call them, you just want to know if you should use them, right? When you research this topic, you'll find articles that support their use and others that call them dangerous. I believe the truth lies somewhere in between. Unfortunately, there's not a lot of science to back up either claim.

Manufacturers of hydrogel products will tout their product's water retentive capacity and claim that they redistribute moisture to the plant roots as needed so you don't have to water as frequently. The jury is still out whether these claims, well, hold water.

According to the typical manufacturer, most of these beads last for approximately three years. This indicates to me that they are constantly eroding and releasing a bit of whatever chemicals they're made of into the soil. Even if they are degrading, there are no studies telling us whether or not the plant roots are uptaking (absorbing) those chemicals. Likewise, if the plant is absorbing them, will they harm us? The fact is, we don't yet know. Personally, if I can't get the answers to these questions, I won't use them on edible plants.

You can use pH test strips to easily, cheaply, and quickly check water quality to make sure it is good for the plants in your hydroponic system or microgreen kit.

Nutrients

Plants receive much-needed carbon, hydrogen, and oxygen from the air and water. Other elements needed for good plant growth come from the soil. As we've discussed earlier, the nutrient content of soil can vary wildly.

The three primary nutrients needed by your plants are nitrogen, phosphorus, and potassium, but plants need secondary nutrients and micronutrients as well. These classifications mean that plants need a larger volume of primary nutrients, less of the secondary, and the least amount of the micronutrients for good growth. Check out the sidebar on the right for more about nitrogen, phosphorus, and potassium.

The three secondary nutrients are calcium, magnesium, and sulfur. They're essential for plant growth, but plants use comparatively smaller amounts of these than the primary nutrients. Calcium helps in cell wall development. Magnesium is involved in photosynthesis and actually moves from the older leaves to the younger ones as needed. Sulfur is essential in the development of chlorophyll and also for protein synthesis.

The seven micronutrients that plants need in trace amounts are boron, chloride, copper, iron, manganese, molybdenum, and zinc. The functions and benefits are too numerous to list here; just know that each one plays a role in plant growth, development, and health. Don't worry too much about the secondary and trace elements unless your plant is showing signs of deficiency.

Many online seed sellers provide the optimal pH ranges for individual plants on their sites. One good example is Johnny's Selected Seeds (*www.johnnyseeds.com*). If you choose one of their sprouting broccoli varieties and look at the "Growing Information" area, you'll see that they prefer a pH between 6 and 7.5.

While a pH test kit is great for checking your water, I like using the 3-in-1 meter to periodically test the soil. In case you don't remember, the 3-in-1 meter checks for light, moisture, and pH.

Although chlorine and pH are chemical factors to know about, the bigger threat to your indoor garden is overwatering and underwatering. While most people are concerned with not giving their plants enough water, far and away, more plants are lost from overwatering. Signs of overwatering can be confusing, especially when the plant droops, as this could also be a sign that the plant is thirsty. Another confusing sign is leaves turning brown or yellow or even falling off the plant. All of these can also be signs of pest or disease problems. The best advice I can give is to use a moisture meter or stick your finger a couple inches (about 5cm) down into the growing medium near each plant every couple of days. If it's moist, don't water even if the top of the soil looks and feels dry.

I like using liquid kelp fertilizer because it's natural, good for all stages of a plant's growth, and sustainable.

NITROGEN (N), PHOSPHORUS (P), AND POTASSIUM (K)

You may remember from science class that nitrogen, phosphorus and potassium are abbreviated as N, P and K on the periodic table of elements. When looking at a bag of fertilizer, whether organic or synthetic, you'll see three numbers, i.e., 10-10-10, 5-10-30, etc. These show the percentage of each of these three main elements, with the remainder of the whole being some kind of filler. The fillers are added so that you can more easily apply the proper amount and don't damage the plant by using too much in a concentrated area.

Nitrogen (N): This is the element that plants need the most for good leaf development. If you see yellowish or pale leaves, a nitrogen deficiency is the first, but not the only, thing to suspect. Be aware that too much nitrogen can hinder certain crops. There's nothing worse than a big, bushy tomato plant with no fruit on it.

Phosphorus (P): Root stimulation, blooming, and fruiting are three of the functions of phosphorus. Animal manures are a source of organic phosphorus. As you can imagine, using fresh manures in your indoor garden wouldn't be a great idea. When choosing a commercially available organic fertilizer, look for low-odor options. Too little phosphorus is usually indicated by "reddening" of leaves. Even after you correct the problem, the leaves can take months to green up, so the best indication of success is seeing new, green growth.

Potassium (K): Potassium helps your plant resist disease, grow stronger stems, and even tolerate drought better. There are several forms of potassium; if you use one that contains potassium chloride, be aware that this is a salt and can do damage to your growing medium if too much is used. Typical signs of potassium deficiency are brown "scorching" on the edges of the leaves, curling of the leaf tips, and yellowing between the leaf's veins.

Yellowing leaves can be a sign of nitrogen deficiency.

Reddening of leaves is a possible sign of phosphorus deficiency.

Browning around the edges of leaves could indicate potassium deficiency.

Using too much fertilizer can be more harmful than using too little. There are several signs of overfertilization, such as discolored or deformed leaves.

While organic fertilizers are great, they're slow-acting. If your soil is deficient in something, you may need a boost of a synthetic fertilizer.

Fertilizers

Before we delve into fertilizers in detail, a word of caution: Don't be too quick to fertilize! Not every plant problem is from a lack of fertilizer, and you can do a tremendous amount of harm if you overfertilize— adding too much of any element(s) when there's not a deficiency can harm your plant and even ruin your soil for months or years. It's especially hard to tell in a hydroponic system if elements are missing. You'll need to research the telltale signs of an individual crop's deficiency based on clues such as pale leaves. For soil-based systems, you don't want to add anything unless you've had the soil tested.

For testing, check with your nearest agricultural university—it likely runs your state's Extension Service. Just search "Extension Service _____" (filling your state's name in the blank). If you're using a soilless mix, make sure they also analyze non-soil and not just soil-based mixes. (In fact, your state's Extension Service is a terrific resource for everything gardening. Become familiar with their website and/or social media.)

TOMATO MYTHS

When you're growing tomatoes, everyone tells you to use Epsom salts for magnesium and powdered eggshells for calcium because tomatoes need both. First of all, the calcium from eggshells isn't usable by the tomato plant. Second, add magnesium and calcium only if your soil is deficient. Adding these elements when the soil already has enough can be detrimental both to the plant short-term and to the soil long-term. Just like overwatering, overfertilizing is worse for the plant than underfertilizing.

Inorganic (Chemical) and Organic Fertilizers

There's a huge debate over whether you should choose to use organic or inorganic (chemical) fertilizers. You will need to decide what's right for you and your family. In a nutshell, organic fertilizers are great, but they are slow-acting. They are best used to build soil before the planting season to prevent nutrient deficiencies and for routine feeding. They do a good job of building your soil fertility.

Inorganic (a.k.a. chemical) fertilizers act faster than organic fertilizers. Chemical fertilizers are the best option when your plant needs a quick boost of nutrients because of a soil deficiency or if you experience a pest or disease problem and the plant has weakened. In general, they are safe to use, and most don't contain petroleum products. Plus, since they are manufactured to precise standards, it's easier to know the exact ratio of the different nutrients and the source of those nutrients.

Quick-Release and Slow-Release Fertilizers

Fast-acting/quick-release fertilizers will likely be inorganic, since organic fertilizers usually act quite slowly. The purpose is to give your plant a quick boost of nutrients that will only last a short period of time—perhaps a week or two.

Slow- or controlled-release fertilizers are meant to make a smaller amount of nutrients available over an extended period of time—usually two or three months. If you insist on only using organic fertilizers, focus on building a great soil ahead of time, and rely on slow-release organic fertilizers to maintain a nutritious environment during your growing season.

Dry, Water-Soluble, and Liquid Fertilizers

Types of dry fertilizers include granules, solid sticks, or tablets. Some granules are meant to be used dry and sprinkled on top of or mixed in with the soil. The solid sticks (a.k.a. spikes) and tablets are also simple to use—you just place the recommended number of sticks or tablets in the soil close to the plant, and they slowly disintegrate every time you water.

Water-soluble fertilizer is a dry fertilizer that is meant to be dissolved in water to form a liquid fertilizer.

Liquid fertilizers come in ready-to-use strength or concentrated strength that must be diluted before use. Check manufacturer's directions whether the liquid fertilizer you're using is meant to drench the soil or be sprayed directly on the leaves. Common organic liquid fertilizers are fish emulsion or liquid kelp fertilizers. When using indoors, check for brands that say they are "low odor"—trust me, this is important.

Dry fertilizers often come in sticks like these that you simply push into the soil.

Final Fertilizer Tips

- If your crop is primarily eaten for its fruits (tomatoes, eggplants, peppers, etc.), use a fertilizer lower in nitrogen (a smaller "N" number), because higher N encourages leaf growth rather than fruit production.
- Many fertilizers can be used in a variety of ways, so always check the manufacturer's directions and use accordingly. For instance, the directions may say something like, "Use full strength once a month or use half strength every two weeks." My preference for more consistent fertilizing is to use half-strength fertilizer more often.
- Say it again with me: overuse of fertilizers is more harmful to your plants and soil than underuse! Get that soil tested to see *if* there are deficiencies, then address these problems individually.

Soil acidifiers that change the pH of soil, including sulfur, are considered amendments.

Let's talk fertilizer, amendments, and compost. Choosing the right ones can be a bit more challenging for indoor gardeners because, unlike in outdoor gardening, you will want to be more cognizant of odors. Here are the definitions of each, but be aware there is quite a bit of crossover between the three.

Fertilizers provide a combination of primary, secondary, and micronutrients to the soil, and thus the plants, but don't necessarily address soil texture. Different products are manufactured to cater to different types of plants—lawns, trees, leafy vegetables, fruiting vegetables, and a whole host of different types of flowers.

Amendments, in general, are used to improve the soil texture by creating pockets for air and water. They also give plant roots space to grow and become stronger. Amendments include things like bone meal, blood meal,

compost, lime, peat moss, perlite, and vermiculite. (We've discussed these in more detail in the Soil section of this chapter.) Soil acidifiers are also lumped into the amendments category. However, they don't change the soil structure but rather the pH level of the soil. They can be found in solid stick or tablet form for use with acid-loving plants like blueberries. Be careful using blood and bone meal indoors, as they can attract your pets or even rodents. I personally find the odor unpleasant when used indoors.

Compost is a mixture comprised of decomposed and recycled organic materials. There's a huge debate: some say compost is solely a soil amendment, while others think of it as a fertilizer. Those in the amendment camp say it doesn't provide any nutrients but plays a valuable role in allowing the nutrients in fertilizer to be more available to plants. Because of my years teaching Square Foot Gardening (SFG), I personally feel that a well-made compost provides nutrients to the plant while *also* acting as an amendment.

I'll explain why. SFG is an outdoor growing method where you grow vegetables, herbs, and flowers in 12" x 12" (30 x 30cm) squares inside of a raised bed using Mel's Mix™, which is a soil-less growing medium that contains peat moss (or coco coir), coarse vermiculite, and a great blended compost composed of at least five different ingredients. SFG does not use any additional fertilizer, and plants grow quite well without it. Each time a square foot is harvested, gardeners add an extra trowel of blended compost. No additional fertilizers or amendments are used unless gardeners encounter a problem. In all the years I've done SFG, I've only occasionally added a little fertilizer on heavy feeders like tomatoes. If compost didn't have nutrients, why would our crops grow so well?

You can learn more about composting in Chapter 13.

A sunny window may generate more heat than cool-season crops can take. I had to move this lettuce farther from the window to a shadier location.

A heat mat can supply supplemental heat not only for seedlings and sprouts, but also for vegetables that need a lot of it.

Warmth

I almost forgot to include this section, because the indoors is a climate-controlled environment. Then I thought about it: when you're planning your outdoor garden, you must take into account the time of year you're growing and either grow cool-season or warm-season crops.

If you tend to like more of the cool-season veggies, such as lettuces, greens, root vegetables, brassicas, peas, etc., you'll need to make sure the area where you're growing them doesn't get too hot. When you're planning where to grow them, remember that these crops are also the ones that usually thrive in less light, so you'll find that a south-southeast-facing window might be the best location, as they will get the milder morning sun.

You may need to be ready with sheer, gauzy curtains that can be utilized during the summer season. If it is still too hot for your cool-loving plants, perhaps you can direct your air conditioning vent toward them or supplement with a fan to keep them cooler.

Conversely, save your south- and southwest-facing window space for those veggies that crave more sun and heat, such as your tomatoes, peppers, and eggplants, because the extra light will tend to create a warmer environment. If it's still not warm enough for them, you can set the pots directly on a heat mat that's used to start seeds.

Note: Everything in the preceding paragraphs is opposite in the southern hemisphere, so be aware of this if you're located below the equator. If you are close to the equator, between the Tropic of Cancer and the Tropic of Capricorn, other than protecting your food or being housebound, there's probably not much reason to grow indoors. If you'd still like to grow indoors, you might need to use the strategies in Chapter 4 to see how to handle your overabundance of sunshine.

PART 3

INDOOR GROWING METHODS

This part of the book will help you decide which method or methods for growing will be best for you and your space. There's no way to cover everything you could possibly need to know, but you'll certainly have a great start when you do your own research and finally set out to purchase what you need.

We'll cover several soil-based and hydroponic methods so that you'll have a good understanding of the advantages and disadvantages of each. For example, a small vertical hydroponic kit might be best if you want to stick to growing a lot of lettuces and greens and are concerned about the weight of a soil-based container system. But if your house is on a slab and you want to grow more things like root vegetables and peppers, then a soil-based system will probably be your choice.

The more you learn about each method, and the more homework you do before buying a system, the less likely you are to make a costly mistake when choosing.

Take the time to choose which method(s) will work best for you.

CHAPTER 7
Container Gardening

A good, soil-based container garden is a versatile option for indoor gardening.

Container gardening is in many ways self-explanatory. It's a soil-based growing method that grows your chosen crops in a pot or some other container of sufficient depth that has adequate drainage and is filled with a good, nutritious growing medium.

Vertical gardening is a form of container gardening vital to indoor gardening. Growing *up* rather than *out* is an important space saver. Refer to Chapter 9 for specific instructions.

Choosing the correct container, and filling it with the right soil, may be a bit more confusing. Of course, if you want to grow long root vegetables like carrots, your container needs to be deep enough to accommodate the length of the variety of carrot you choose. If you're growing shallow-rooted veggies like lettuce or greens, then your container can be shallower.

No matter what, your container must have a sufficient number of holes in the bottom that offer good drainage, or the roots will rot and the plant will eventually die. But that means you also need to have something under the pot to catch the extra water so it doesn't damage your floor or table.

Materials

You can choose any number of natural materials for your indoor containers, such as terracotta, stone, or metal. However, if weight is a concern, which it will be for many readers and home gardeners, there are really only a few logical choices: plastic, resin, or foam. I try to limit the amount of plastic I use, but it's just a fact that it is the best and most readily available choice for indoor gardening. A sturdy plastic container is a one-time purchase, and many times you can repurpose things you already have in the house as containers to reduce your waste, consumption, and costs.

Plastic

As long as you're careful when choosing a container, plastic is a great option for indoor gardening. Plastic containers are inexpensive and lightweight, last forever, and are available in many styles and colors to coordinate with your décor.

What constitutes a safe plastic for indoor gardening? Basically, it's one that doesn't chip, off-gas, or contain toxic chemicals that, if they deteriorate, might seep into your growing medium. There is so much information, and

misinformation, out there about using plastic containers when growing food. You may have heard that plastics should be avoided altogether because the chemicals leach into the soil. That's not necessarily true.

Almost anything can be used as a gardening container, but be aware of the weight.

A tomato plant thriving in a DIY plastic container. The clear plastic can be a nifty aesthetic choice!

Look for the numbers 2, 4, 1, and 5 on plastics you plan to use for growing food.

On the bottom of any plastic object, you should see a stylized triangle with a number in the middle, which is recognized as the universal recycling symbol. The numbers refer to different types or grades of plastic. Don't get bogged down by researching and memorizing all the many numbers for different types of plastic. You only need to remember these four numbers: 2, 4, 1, and 5. And they're in that order for a reason! Basically, if the container once held food, it's generally safe to grow in. While numbers 2, 4, 1, and 5 are all safe for the indoor or outdoor garden, I've listed them in order starting with the safest. No other plastic containers should be used when growing food.

If you love science or want a little more information, here are the four safe plastics, along with some items you may already have in your home:

#2—High-Density Polyethylene (HDPE): The biggest benefits of #2 plastic are that it resists ultraviolet (UV) light and very hot temperatures without transmitting chemicals into the soil. The most common item you'll run into is a plastic milk container. It's the best choice for growing food.

#4—Low-Density Polyethylene (LDPE): This is another great choice for gardening, as it is not known to transmit chemicals even when exposed to high heat. You will find LDPE used in many food storage containers.

#1—Polyethylene Terephthalate (PET/PETE): This plastic is the most commonly recycled. The issue with using PET in the garden is that it tends to break down with long-term exposure to light or heat. You'll find this used in containers like soda bottles and plastic food jars. Of course, with indoor gardening, you're not subjecting the material to light and heat as intensely as you would outdoors, so it's a good choice.

#5—Polypropylene (PP): I've included #5 in the list because it is regarded as safe and is an acceptable choice for gardening; it is found in food containers. Since there *might* be a slight chance of leaching, it's not my first choice.

Want to make sure you remember these four numbers without fail? Numbers are easier to remember when they're grouped together and when you say them out loud. So, think of the best types of plastic, #2 and #4, collectively as twenty-four, and the acceptable types, #1 and #5, as fifteen. Then say them out loud a few times to reinforce the memory!

PLASTICS IN HYDROPONIC SYSTEMS

While we're talking about plastics, let's quickly cover polyvinyl chloride (PVC), which matters when it comes to hydroponic systems (more on these in Chapter 8). PVC pipes used for hydroponics fall into a different category than normal plastics, since hydroponics is not considered a container gardening method. You do need to look carefully for food-safe PVC when choosing a hydroponic system. Look specifically for the words "food safe" or UPVC.

Where people get into trouble using PVC is not from the pipes and couplings, but in the overuse of the cleaner and glue that holds them together. Technically you're using pipe cement and primer, but it's commonly called glue and cleaner. Unlike adhesives, when applied, PVC cement breaks down the external layers of the pipe and fitting, permanently bonding them together. You get one chance to do this, so make sure the fittings are aligned correctly before pushing the pipe into it. You will never be able to separate the two pieces.

Most hydroponic systems can be dry fit and don't need any glue at all. If you don't trust that your system won't leak, carefully apply the cleaner and glue only where they actually meet, and don't use too much.

Foam and resin containers are great, lightweight options and can blend easily with your decor.

Resin containers can look like wood, cement, marble, and more. They are incredibly sturdy, yet light.

Resin and Foam

Resin is a composite material that is usually made of #4 LDPE plastic and other ingredients that make it resist fading, cracking, and breaking. It starts as a powder that is liquefied, colored, and poured into a mold that can mimic things like stone or metal, but it weighs considerably less than those materials.

Polystyrene foam containers are extremely lightweight. While the National Institutes of Health (NIH) classifies styrene as a carcinogen, that warning is for those working around it in the manufacturing process, not for those drinking from a Styrofoam cup or planting in foam containers. Because you are growing indoors where the containers are not exposed to high heat, and because the material takes many years to break down, it should not be of concern. However, if you are at all apprehensive about using foam containers, do your own research and make the decision that's best for you and your family.

Container Width, Depth, and Drainage

In Chapter 6, we talked about what plants need, and I mentioned that overwatering is a common reason for plant death. Being mindful that your containers have the proper amount of drainage and that your soil doesn't hold too much water is critical.

At the same time, your containers need to be the proper width and depth to hold the plant's roots plus allow for a sufficient amount of soil. In addition to a root ball, some

plants send out a long main vertical root called a taproot. The taproot's purpose is to go down deep into the soil to reach nutrients and moisture. Because we're providing nutrients and moisture in the container, it's not as much of a concern as when growing outdoors. For instance, tomatoes have a taproot that, when planted outdoors, will go straight down about 5' (1.5m). However, when grown in a container, that taproot

Consider what you're growing when figuring out how deep your containers need to be. For example, carrots need deep pots, whereas lettuces don't.

will happily grow and curl around in the pot. Just be sure the container is of sufficient size so that the plant does not become root-bound, meaning that because the roots are too limited, the plant's aboveground growth is also limited.

But what if you want to grow shallow-rooted vegetables in a deep container? That's fine, but if weight is a concern, the solution is to fill the bottom few inches (about 5cm) with a super-lightweight material such as perlite, vermiculite, or coco coir and then using your growing medium for the top 4"–6" (11–15cm). I've even used peanut hulls from unsalted bulk peanuts to fill in space without adding much weight. The peanuts must be unsalted, as salt can kill your plants!

When possible, it's a good practice to check the drainage before planting. Fill the pot with your intended growing medium, set it onto the tray or saucer, put it in the sink or bathtub, and overwater to see what happens. Does the soil drain well? Are the holes large enough? Are they too large? If you overfill it, does the tray do its job?

If the holes are too small, or there aren't enough of them, you can drill extras or enlarge the existing ones. Empty the container and turn it upside down so that you're drilling from the outside of the pot to the inside. Plastic, resin, and foam pots only need standard drill bits. However, cement, pottery, or porcelain pots will need a more expensive special carbide masonry or diamond drill bit. You'll need to proceed slowly and possibly use water to keep the bit cool. Look online for more thorough instructions on drilling these materials.

After adjusting the holes, do the drainage test again before planting. If you notice a lot of soil draining out of the pot, cut window screening material and place it in the bottom of the pot to hold the soil in.

To stop excess water from damaging surfaces, place plastic trays or glazed ceramic saucers underneath each pot, or group containers together into a larger tray such as a cat litter box (unused, of course!), cement mixing tub, aluminum chafing pans, or anything else you may have around the house. I stress using only glazed ceramic saucers because unglazed (i.e., terra cotta) saucers are porous and will allow moisture to escape, creating the possibility of damage to the table or floor surface below.

This is also a great strategy if you have plants that like extra moisture, especially during the dry winter months. Put an inch or two (2–5cm) of gravel in the bottom of the tray and add water to the top of the gravel. Place several pots on top, and they'll benefit from the moistened air.

Container Types and Locations

Windows and Windowsills

Using windows or windowsills helps lighten the load on your floors and saves floor space. There are several suction cup–style shelf and planter systems available commercially that can attach right to a window without a sill. Check online reviews to make sure other buyers are satisfied with the performance of the suction cups. Take note of the maximum weight of the unit, and make sure your containers are lightweight and filled with a lightweight growing medium. Don't forget to factor in the mature weight of the plant plus the water. Shelves must be level to ensure the planters don't slide off. If you're in an area prone to earthquakes, using museum putty (a type of non-damaging adhesive putty) can help stabilize them.

Growing on a windowsill is simple: just find an appropriate-sized container of your choice that fits safely on your windowsill. It should have a hole or holes for proper drainage and something below it to collect any excess water to protect the sill from water damage. Using rectangular or long, slightly oval-shaped planters, rather than round containers, will make the most of your space and be more stable.

Both window and windowsill containers should be deep enough to accommodate the root system of the crops you

Using window and windowsill containers are great ways to grow food indoors.

intend to grow. If the room is especially hot, you will need to provide some shade or cooling.

Give round pots a quarter turn, or rectangular containers a half turn, at least every week, but better yet every other day, to provide even sun exposure to all sides of the plant. This ensures your plants will grow more evenly.

Countertops and Tabletops

If you have bright under-cabinet lights, you'll be able to grow part-shade herbs and lettuces out of the way on your kitchen countertops. Check out the section on supplemental lighting in Chapter 4 to learn more about ensuring you are providing adequate light. When the plants are small, you will want to raise the containers up so that the tops of the plants are just an inch or two (2–5cm) away from the lights, or they may become too leggy and spindly. As the plants grow taller, you will need to lower them so they don't touch the hot lights. If you're able, they will benefit from occasionally spending a few hours in front of a bright window.

If you don't have suitable under-cabinet lights, you can use a small table located near a sunny window to grow herbs, lettuces, and greens in various containers. These crops require much less light. As with windowsill growing, the depth of the container will depend on the depth of the plant's root system; adequate drainage is vital. Protecting your table surface can be as simple as using containers with trays, but I suggest adding a waterproof table covering. You can purchase tabletop supplemental lights, some with multiple arms and fixtures to cover multiple pots.

If you don't have a lot of room to grow indoors, some herbs on the kitchen counter or tabletop are ideal.

Freestanding Units

There are various tall freestanding growing systems that can be purchased and used indoors, but they can be quite heavy, and you may need to modify them to protect your floor from water damage.

Some plants can be grown in pots on shelves such as bookshelves as long as you can reach in easily to tend to them.

One thing I've used for several years to grow a little food indoors and start seeds for my outdoor garden is an old shoe tower. It has rods that give me the perfect angle for maximum sun exposure. I've removed every other row of rods to give me adequate space as the plants get taller. Since it's on wheels, I'm able to move it to follow the sun.

A shoe tower makes an economical DIY holder for some containers. Just remove every other "shelf" to give plants more room.

You may be able to turn your pots within the unit to give the plants more or less sun.

If your budget allows, this Garden Tower 2 is a great option. Optional light kits are available.

A lazy Susan plus stackable planters makes an affordable vertical growing system.

To grow shallow-rooted veggies on that shoe tower, I've turned safe plastic shoe storage boxes into wicking containers. This was done simply by taking two identical boxes that nest together. Drill a couple holes in the top box to provide drainage, and a couple more to insert either long strips of T-shirt material or wicking cord (from now, on we'll just call these wicks). The second box is left intact to catch excess water. You should put something like plastic bottle caps or a few marbles in the bottom of this second box to act as spacers. Through two of the holes of the top box, thread the wicks so that they hang down a few inches (about 7cm) and lay on the floor of the second box, then nest the two boxes. Gently hold the other end of the wicks, being careful not to pull them out, while you fill the top box, a little at a time, with damp growing medium.

This is a good time to explain the mechanics of the wicking container. Unlike a self-watering container where you fill a bottom reservoir, you will add extra water to the soil in the top box, and the bottom box will capture that excess. When needed by the plants, the wicks will draw the water from the bottom box into the top box. The goal is to have the wicking material snaking through the soil so that it is consistently moist. As you fill the box, allow the wick to rest at different levels and in different areas so that there is good coverage within the box. This type of container is particularly suited for plants that like constant moisture, such as mint, peas, watercress, and spinach, as well as many lettuces and greens.

Creating maximum growing space using a minimal footprint is important when you live in an apartment or small house and is best accomplished by growing vertically whenever possible.

Hanging planters are great for small spaces.

Far and away, my favorite large-scale freestanding container is the Garden Tower 2. I participated in their crowdfunding campaign in 2014. The system is a round planter about 30" (76cm) in diameter and about 42" (107cm) in height with forty-five planting holes along the side with room for more plants on the top. It rotates 360 degrees and captures excess water in a bin. It also has a perforated tube in the center where you can compost garden and kitchen scraps and even add worms to speed up the process. I don't personally use the compost tube indoors, but I know people who do.

If this isn't in your budget, you can mimic the idea by using a stackable planter with a tray on top of a sturdy lazy Susan.

Hanging Planters

When choosing hanging planters, of course, like windowsill and tabletop growing, you need to be concerned about adequate sun exposure, container depth, drainage, and drip trays. Choose your hanging container wisely. Most are made solely for outdoor use and have drainage holes but no tray underneath. Hanging basket drip pans are widely available online and at garden stores.

Another good choice is a self-watering hanging planter so that you won't have to water as frequently. To do this, place a medium like coco coir or hydroponic pebbles in the bottom of the basket before filling it with soil. This will create a reservoir for the water. They typically have an easy fill area and a visible water indicator.

Small hanging planters can be hooked onto a sturdy curtain rod, but it's most common to use hooks that screw into the ceiling. Be sure to find a ceiling joist or use drywall anchors to hold the hook securely to the ceiling. If you have a drop ceiling, there are special hooks that can be fastened to the metal cross pieces.

Always utilize a lightweight growing medium when using hanging baskets indoors, rotate the plants at least weekly for even sun exposure, and don't forget those drip trays.

CHAPTER 8

Hydroponic Gardening

Instead of soil, hydroponic systems often use a substrate like this spongy rock wool block.

Clay pellets are another substrate used in hydroponics. They are set inside of a plastic basket called a net or net pot.

Look at the strong roots of this beautiful lettuce growing out of the plastic net pot!

There's a learning curve with any new growing method, but especially with hydroponics. Because there's so much to learn, I won't be able to go through these methods in any great detail, but I will give you the basics of what to look for if you want to dive into hydroponics. To be honest, once this book was written and the photographs taken, I dismantled my small hydroponics set and put it away. They're great for people growing a single crop, but it was not worth it to me to grow much in my nutrient film system, which you'll learn about shortly.

Other than the small plug-and-play systems discussed below, I do not recommend hydroponic systems for beginner gardeners unless you're willing to devote a lot of time to learning more about them. That said, hydroponics can be rewarding, so don't let my reservations discourage you if you are interested.

All hydroponic systems need to provide three things to the plant for healthy growth: water, nutrients, and oxygen. Systems are classified as either active or passive. In general, active means that the nutrient solutions (water and nutrients) are moved to the plant through the use of a pump, while passive systems rely on a wick to move the solutions.

Hydroponic systems are further broken down into two additional categories: recovery and non-recovery. With recovery systems, the nutrient solution is recirculated by a pump and is reused. Non-recovery systems mean that the solution is applied to the growing medium and then vanishes. Think of non-recovery systems like a traditional soil-based system where you water the plants once and then have to do it over and over again. Of course, you'll add more nutrient solution to a recovery system periodically, but not as frequently as to a non-recovery system.

Types of Systems

Let's quickly look at some of the different hydroponic systems available and what types of crops can be grown in each.

Wick system: The wick system is the simplest because it's a passive system that doesn't require electricity. Plants are placed in an absorbent growing medium like perlite, coco coir, or a rigid substrate. A wick made of various materials,

In a wick system, an absorbent material hangs down into the nutrient solution and draws it up to moisten and feed the roots of the plant.

This deep water culture (DWC) system requires a deep tank (reservoir) for the nutrient solution and an air pump to provide oxygen to the roots.

Aeroponics

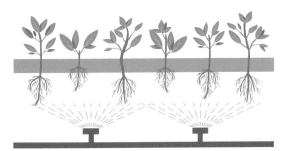

Deep Water Culture

Drip System

Nutrient Film Technique

These cut-away drawings clearly show the mechanics of four of the six main types of hydroponic growing. Read on for more detail about each.

such as nylon or cotton, runs from the plant roots into a reservoir filled with a nutrient solution. The best plants for a wick system are those that don't require too much water to grow well, like lettuces and herbs. I've heard this is a good system in which to grow your rosemary, but you'll need to spray the rosemary leaves a few times a week to mimic its native environment.

Deep water culture system: This is one of the most popular hydroponic systems because almost all types of plants can be grown with it. In this system, the plant's roots are suspended fully in the nutrient solution, and an air pump and an air stone are used to provide oxygen to the roots. This is an easy DIY system to create. Good crop choices include lettuces, greens, and any water-loving crops. Since this system is basically a "raft," you'll want to choose crops that aren't top-heavy, unless you provide support. For

instance, if you'd like to grow vining tomatoes, you'll need to wind twine around the main stem and connect it to the ceiling so the vines grow vertically.

Nutrient film technique: With the nutrient film technique, slightly sloped PVC pipes have the nutrient solution pumped up from a reservoir and flow over the plant's root systems. In this active recovery system, the solution then loops back down to the reservoir, where it is again pumped upward. Instead of a typical growing medium, NFT systems often use sponges or small clay balls inside of a net pot (net cup) to hold the plant root securely. When I hear the word "net," I immediately think of a flexible woven rope structure used for fishing or a butterfly net made of mesh. However, the net pot is more like a rigid plastic basket with very large openings. The technique is best suited for growing any short-season plants like lettuces and greens.

This nutrient film technique (NFT) system encourages the plant roots to grow long to access the shallow film of nutrient solution at the bottom half of the PVC pipe while allowing the top part of the roots to breathe.

Here's an example of an aeroponic system where the blue-tipped emitter sprays the nutrient solution directly on the plant roots. If a plant starts to look bad, make sure the emitter is not clogged. Cleaning emitters is a weekly chore with this method.

It's also good for herbs like mint and basil, and it's even good for strawberries.

Ebb and flow system (a.k.a. flood and drain): In this system, you place plants into a large growing tray filled with a growing medium such as coco coir, clay balls, etc. The nutrient solution is flooded onto the grow tray from a large reservoir, left for a certain amount of time, and then drained back into the reservoir. The draining period allows the growing medium to dry out somewhat. Often a timer is used for this flooding and draining. It is a good system for growing almost anything, including large plants like cucumbers, tomatoes, and beans.

Drip systems: These are simple to set up and use. The nutrient solution is pumped directly to the base of the plant and an emitter allows the solution to drip at the desired rate, which saturates the growing medium. You can grow almost any type of plant in a drip system.

Aeroponics: This is not the easiest method. Basically, plants are suspended above the reservoir that holds the nutrient solution and the solution is sprayed over the plants' roots. Almost any type of plant can be grown with this system, including tomatoes and strawberries, but the mist nozzles must be kept clean and frequently adjusted to ensure that the entire root system is kept moist.

Plug-and-Play Systems

There are a number of plug-and-play growing appliances on the market that combine watering, nutrient delivery, and supplemental lighting and which require minimal weekly care. Some come with pre-seeded pods that you just pop into the device and off it goes! A few fancy "smart systems" are available that have WiFi connectivity and a corresponding app for your smartphone to tell you when the appliance needs attention.

As always, convenience comes with a price tag. The plug-and-play systems that have pre-seeded pods are great, but replacement pods can be pricy. They usually have options for unseeded pods where you can grow your own seeds.

These strawberries are growing great in this drip system, which uses a growing medium along with a drip irrigation system.

DIY HYDROPONIC JAR

Kids love to watch things grow, and here's a fun way to introduce them to a simple hydroponics system loosely based on the Kratky method, which is a simplified version of the deep water culture method described on page 80. Close adult supervision is needed for this project—it's a project to be done together, not for kids to do alone.

Materials and Tools
- Small glass canning jar (with either a solid lid or a two-piece ring/band and lid)
- Plastic hydroponic basket (sometimes called nets)
- Substrate material of your choice, e.g., clay hydroponic balls, pressed peat moss cone (used in this example), hydroponic sponge, etc.
- Drill with a hole saw bit that's slightly smaller than the basket (or see alternative to the right of step 2)
- Hammer and small nail or awl
- Water
- Liquid fertilizer
- Seeds or a small transplant (leaf lettuce, snap peas, basil, or marigold are easy to grow)

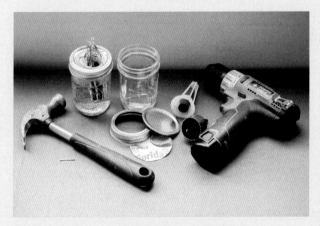

You don't need many materials or tools to make this!

Note: For the rosemary pictured, I took a cutting from an established plant, cut a slit along the side of a pressed peat cone, and laid the woody cutting in the slit. Rosemary likes to have its needles sprayed a couple times a week. This is an especially slow growing plant.

Instructions

1 Prepare for the hole. If you have a drill with a hole saw bit, use the hammer to tap the small nail or awl gently to make a dimple in the center of the lid. This will help guide the hole saw bit, which you will use to make a hole in the lid to hold the plastic hydroponic basket.

3 Set up the basket. Place your substrate material of choice in the hydroponic basket and put the basket into the lid hole. Check the fit, then remove the lid and basket from the jar temporarily.

2 Drill the hole. Use the drill to make a hole in the lid. The hole should be slightly smaller than the basket so that the basket will sit snugly inside it without falling in.

If you don't have access to a drill and hole saw bit, you can use a canning jar with a ring/band and a piece of thin, waxy paperboard from a milk or juice carton instead of the metal jar lid. Simply cut the paperboard into a circle to fit nicely into the ring/band, then cut a hole into the circle to fit the basket.

Congrats! You've made a mini hydroponics system. Keep an eye on the water level and add as needed; fertilize on the schedule your plant needs.

4 Add the water, nutrients, and plant. Fill the jar half full with water. Follow the liquid fertilizer dilution directions, add it to the water, and stir well. Then screw on the lid with the basket and substrate, and plant your seeds. If you are using a transplant with enough roots that will stabilize the plant, you won't have to use the substrate. If the transplant has been grown in soil, gently wash off as much of the growing medium from the roots as possible.

This jar is a fun project for all ages, not just for kids.

I used the smaller model Click and Grow like the one shown on the table behind the man in this photo; the larger Smart Garden 9 that he's holding would be ideal for most families.

There are many plug-and-play systems on the market, with AeroGarden being one of the pioneers. Mine was a tiny tabletop model with just three pods (smaller than the one pictured).

One such product is the Smart Garden by Click and Grow. When I contacted them to talk about plug-and-play systems, they offered to send one to me. I chose to test the smallest model available, the Smart Garden 3. It measures approximately 4¾" x 12" (12 x 30.5cm) and looks quite tidy on my kitchen counter. It couldn't have been simpler: load the pods, add water, and plug it in. It costs $99.95; larger models go for upwards of $200.

Initially, you put little domes over the individual pods to act as mini greenhouses to help with germination, and you remove them as the plants break the soil. The attached lamp starts out close to the plants, and you add arm extensions to raise it as they grow. Keep an eye on the water level indicator and don't refill it until a few days after the indicator reaches the bottom to allow the pod to dry out a bit.

This system is not just for growing leafy greens and herbs—pods are available for peppers, mini tomatoes, wild strawberries, and flowers. You can purchase replacement pods in packs of three or nine, and there's an option to join their Plant Plan subscription program for a reduced price.

The only problem I've run into with this product is that sometimes, if the box of pods gets bumped or turned upside down during transport, the seeds may fall out. That's not a problem if you buy a pack with the same type of seed in it, but I got a pack with three pods each of peppers, tomatoes, and strawberries. Luckily, I was able to identify which seeds went with each pod. The company will replace any pod that doesn't germinate.

The time-honored AeroGarden is another example of a small tabletop plug-and-play system. You can also find larger systems like those from Rise Gardens that look like a stylish piece of furniture. In addition to small tabletop units, Click and Grow and AeroGarden offer larger, vertical models, so there are several options from which to choose. These are by no means the only options on the market, so look online to find a system that you like and that fits your décor. Although I haven't used Rise Gardens personally, I like the sleek looks of their blond wood and white Family Gardens. They come complete with grow lights for each level, and I like that the lights have sides on them so that they don't blind you. I appreciate the large water reservoir and storage area on the bottom too.

Whatever brand you choose, there are sure to be online videos that show you the unboxing, installation process, and reviews of each to help you make the best decisions. One factor to consider is noise. The sound of water flowing through the various systems reminds me of a soothing fountain, but it might annoy you if it's in the same room as your television.

Special Considerations

Fertilizing

Because your plants won't get the same nutrients, especially micronutrients, that they'd get from a good soil, you need to be sure to use the correct nutrient solution made specifically for hydroponics. Fertilizers can be purchased dry and will then be mixed with water, or in liquid form—either ready to use or as a concentrate that you mix with water. See Chapter 6 under the Nutrients section for more information about primary and secondary nutrients.

The Importance of pH

When using a hydroponic system, you need to closely monitor the pH level of the water. The ideal range for most plants is between 5.5 and 6.5. The pH level affects nutrient availability for your plants. If the pH level is too high, above 6.5, it is considered alkaline, and this can prevent nutrient uptake and lead to deficiencies, especially in iron. A pH under 5.0 is too basic, and it can result in magnesium and calcium deficiencies or even copper and iron toxicity in the plant.

You will need to have pH paper or a pH meter available and test your water every couple of days. There are easy-to-use commercially available products that are generally named "pH up" and "pH down" that are added to your nutrient solution to help you maintain the right balance for your plants. Note that different plants have different pH requirements.

Source Water

If you use tap water in your hydroponic system, you may have to take several steps to test and modify it before you can use it (read more about this in Chapter 6). If you are growing on a large scale, it's worth your time to study how to get your water ready for use. If like me, you only plan on growing small amounts of your food hydroponically, you can rely on rainwater, distilled water, or deionized water. Consider local laws if you decide to collect rainwater. Search "rainwater harvesting in _____" (filling in your state's name).

There are several types of fertilizers you can use, such as granules that can be mixed into the soil or into water, or this liquid kelp fertilizer. Whatever you use, be sure to follow the directions on the package.

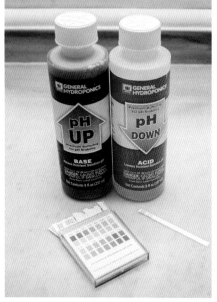

When using a hydroponic system, you'll need a pH testing kit and solutions to quickly raise and lower pH as needed.

Using distilled water is one way to ensure you have complete control of the water quality and that there are no surprise problems in your water.

While the processes for creating each are different, distilled and deionized water both have had all contaminants removed; however, this means you'll need to more carefully check your nutrients. Most commercially available nutrient concentrates have lower amounts of calcium (Ca) and magnesium (Mg) to compensate for their presence in tap water. Although they are needed by plants, too much calcium and magnesium can block the absorption of other nutrients. If this is the case, there are separate Ca/Mg solutions, but don't add too much, or you've just made your water hard again.

It's difficult to offer good specific advice on this topic because your water may be completely different than the water found just a few miles away. It's best to consult a local hydroponics expert.

TDS, PPM, and EC

Another thing you'll need to stay on top of is the TDS, PPM, and EC of your water. I advise you to get a good meter that measures all three.

A meter like this one will allow you to check the nutrient and mineral quality of your water.

TDS = totally dissolved solids
PPM = parts per million
EC = electrical conductivity

The TDS of water has to do with the quantity of dissolved minerals in it and is a loose measure of water quality, but it doesn't guarantee that pollutants aren't present. TDS is measured in parts per million (PPM). According to the World Health Organization (WHO):

- Fresh water has a TDS of less than 1,000 PPM
- Brackish water has a TDS up to 5,000 PPM
- Saline water has a TDS between 15,000–30,000 PPM
- Seawater has a TDS between 30,000–40,000 PPM
- Brine has a TDS above 40,000 PPM

In hydroponics, TDS gives you an idea of the strength of your nutrient solution in PPM. As with pH, different plants have different PPM requirements.

The electrical conductivity (EC) refers to how well the water conducts electricity, which is determined by the amount of minerals dissolved in it. Pure water, water without any minerals dissolved in it, does not conduct electricity, even though water in general is a good conductor of electricity. That is because most water we encounter in our lives does have minerals dissolved in it.

Since the majority of nutrients used in hydroponics involve salts, adding nutrients increases the EC of the water. Knowing the EC gives you an idea of the levels of nutrient concentration in your water. EC is measured in milliSiemens and microSiemens. If your nutrient solution is too dilute, growth won't be as good, and if it's too concentrated, it can lead to toxicity or nutrient lockout. Absorption and transpiration of the nutrients by the plants will change the EC. And, of course, the optimal EC is different for each crop.

The only way to discern that everything is good for your crops is by frequently using a PPM/EC/TDS meter and also measuring the pH with a separate meter or by using pH test strips. It's critical to measure the fresh solution before adding it to your hydroponic system and as the plants grow.

Tips and Troubleshooting

Although Part 5 of this book is also called Tips and Troubleshooting, I felt a separate subsection was needed in this chapter because hydroponics is more difficult than soil-based growing; more can go wrong.

Leaking

Remember I said you can learn from my mistakes? Well, the first mistake I made was not making sure the tubing leading from the pump to the top of the PVC pipes was snugly connected to the nipple. That resulted in a slow drip that dribbled down the tube into the reservoir. It didn't do any damage, but it could have been a big problem if that constant slow drip had landed outside the bin. I used a hairdryer to soften the tubing so that it fit more tightly onto the nipple and stopped the drip.

All fixed, right? Well, I left the room and didn't notice that when I was fixing that little problem, I inadvertently bumped the drain fitting out of place. Instead of the nutrient solution draining nicely back into the reservoir bin . . . you guessed it . . . 2 ½ gallons (9.5L) of nutrient solution went all over my floor. Thankfully, I had a rubber-backed, absorbent rug in the area, but it wasn't designed to absorb that much water. I had to move my *entire* garden, including the large soil-based Garden Tower mentioned earlier, and clean it up. Had I not noticed it right away, it would surely have resulted in major damage to my laminate flooring.

So, be sure that if you work on your hydroponic system, you don't knock something loose or off-kilter. After you make any adjustments, keep a close eye on your system.

Before planting, no matter which type of hydroponics you use, check for leaks. Make sure any bins (reservoirs) you use don't have cracks or holes in them. Check the PVC pipes to ensure they're snug. If they're not, and you've dry fit them, you'll need to glue them. See the sidebar on Safe Plastics in Chapter 7 for hints on cleaning and gluing PVC pipes—don't use too much of either, or you could introduce unsafe chemicals into your system.

I ended up using four large aluminum foil chafing dishes underneath the entire hydroponic system so that even if I have a catastrophic leak, any one of the pans will hold all of the water in the system. Yes, the same chafing dishes you would use at a buffet table to keep your food warm. They are very inexpensive and do a wonderful job of keeping the area protected.

Cleaning, Testing, and Observing

What I didn't realize when I started my hydroponic system is how much upkeep would be involved. The whole system should be drained, flushed, and cleaned every couple of weeks, including the pumps and tubing. I fell down on this task to the detriment of my plants. I admit it—I'm a lazy gardener, which is probably why I'm not a huge hydroponics fan.

You'll need to test the pH frequently, which is why I opted for using a meter instead of test strips. The pH can change quickly for a number of reasons, such as how quickly your plants are absorbing nutrients, the temperature of the room, and, in dry climates, from evaporation of the solution.

Check your plants often for any signs of pest or disease problems and deal with them immediately. Unlike wine, garden problems do not get better with age.

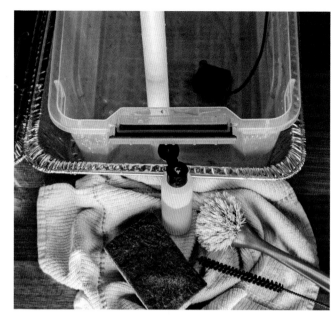

Whether the system is recovery or non-recovery, you will need to drain, flush, and clean your system every few weeks.

Different Crops, Different Growing Requirements

All the plants in a single hydroponic system must have similar nutrient (PPE) needs or you won't be successful. While everything was just right for this New Zealand spinach (the big plant), the tatsoi is definitely not as happy.

Depending on the hydroponic method you're using, you'll need to consider that plants have different pH, PPE, EC, etc. requirements, so make sure that the different crops you're growing in a single system have the same needs. There are several charts available online by searching "hydroponic vegetable needs." You'll need to stay on top of it and organize your system smartly.

CHAPTER 9

Vertical Wall Gardens and Growing Sprouts, Microgreens, and Baby Greens

Wall gardens are essentially container gardens, but they have some special considerations we'll cover in this chapter.

In this chapter, we'll discuss two different miscellaneous methods: wall gardens and growing sprouts, microgreens, and baby greens. Wall gardens are technically a form of container gardening, but they have special considerations that warrant their placement here. And the processes of growing sprouts, microgreens, and baby greens are quite special and specific.

Wall Gardens

There are a variety of plastic wall garden systems available, but this felt wall pocket is a great alternative that's less expensive.

Although wall gardens are actually a type of container garden, in that they hold soil, I'm separating them. They remove some of the weight from the floor, and they allow vining crops to grow vertically downward, which saves space. You have to be careful not to ruin the drywall by overspraying while watering. It will be necessary to drill holes into the wall, which will need to be repaired if you move.

See Chapter 3 for more information about how walls are constructed. One of the things I mentioned there was using a French cleat to hang a wall garden, and that's what I did to hang my wall pocket garden. I also put up a waterproof backing with some thin wooden strips on it to make sure there was air space between the wall pocket and the wall to minimize damage from water.

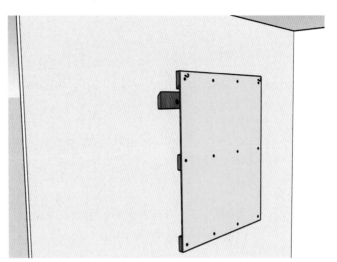

To protect your walls, consider setting your wall pocket garden off from the wall using a French cleat hanger.

Fabric wall pockets are perfect because they're made from felt fabric and weigh almost nothing. Just be sure they are meant for indoor use, which usually means they have a layer of plastic sheeting sewn between the fabric layers.

A good, lightweight growing medium is critical. We talked about PittMoss a little in Chapter 6, and this is my choice for wall pockets. In this case, I specifically like their Plentiful Organic Potting Mix. As mentioned, a 2 cubic foot (0.06 cubic meter) bag weighs around 18 lbs. (8kg), which is incredibly light. In addition to being lightweight, the manufacturer claims it needs two-thirds less water than other soils. I used a little less than 1 cubic foot (0.03 cubic meters) of soil for my 22" x 28" (56 x 71cm) six-pocket wall pocket.

To set up your wall pocket, fill the pockets, making sure you stuff some soil into the bottom corners of each pocket. Don't pack it too tightly, but make sure each pocket bulges out so you know there is enough soil for the plants to grow.

To plant the wall pocket, choose shallow-rooted crops like lettuce, greens, small radishes and turnips, and many herbs. Some varieties of peas and beans are also shallow-rooted. Lightly moisten your growing medium and plant just as you would in any other container. Because this container

Use a long-spouted watering can to precisely water into each pocket to reduce the risk of overspray damaging your walls.

Have you ever wondered what goes on underground when you plant a pea seed? This photo shows different stages of growth.

is made of fabric, the moisture will tend to evaporate a little more quickly, especially if you're using a product designed for outdoor use, so it will require more frequent watering. It's best to use a watering can with a long spout so your watering will be more precise, rather than something like a sprayer. If you do get water on the walls, dry them immediately.

Growing Sprouts, Microgreens, and Baby Greens

If you've ever bought sprouts, microgreens, or baby greens at the grocery store, you won't be surprised that, after herbs and spices, these nutrient powerhouses will give you a very good return on investment. They all have more nutrition per ounce or gram than the mature versions of these veggies and herbs. Best of all, they're easy to grow with or without fancy equipment. They are a great option for indoor growing.

First, let's talk about the difference between each of these. With sprouts, you eat the fully germinated seed after the root starts to form but before the stem comes out of the top of the seed. Think of these as seed babies. No soil is used when sprouting seeds—they are germinated by being soaked and rinsed in water.

Microgreens are the next stage in a plant's development, and we'll think of them as seed toddlers. Microgreens can be harvested when the germinated seeds have developed tiny roots and at least their first true leaves, not just the seed leaves (cotyledon). Some are best grown in water and others in soil.

Finally, baby greens are the pre-teens of seed growing. They are easily identifiable as miniature lettuces or greens, but they are harvested before they are fully formed, when they are still a bit more nutritious than the adult plants and are more tender and sweet.

Sprouts

There are several ways you can grow sprouts—in plastic sprouting trays, in sprout towers, or in cloth sprouting bags. The most common way to grow sprouts is by using glass canning jars with either special draining lids or a couple layers of cheesecloth over the top secured with a rubber band.

However you grow them, *do not* use regular seeds that you would plant in the ground. Look for a reputable source of sprouting seeds; make sure that whatever seed sprouter (container) you use is scrupulously clean. Be sure to follow the directions on the seed packet precisely. See the end of this section for additional warnings before you decide to grow sprouts.

The basics of sprouting, no matter which method you use, are:

- Soak the seeds in fresh water in a sterilized container. Soaking time varies based on variety, so check the seed pack for instruction.
- After soaking, rinse the seeds with clean water and put them into your sprouter.
- Rinse with clean water two or three times a day and drain.
- Most sprouts will be ready to eat in anywhere from three days to two weeks. Rinse and drain one last time.
- Eat immediately or refrigerate and use within a couple days.

This two-part sprouting tray is handy. Larger seeds can be put directly into the white drainage tray and set on top of the green tray filled with water. Cover with plastic food wrap to contain the moisture.

In a canning setup with a draining lid, simply pour water into the jar through the lid, swirl the water around to rinse the seed, and tilt the jar to allow the water to drain.

For a tower setup, basically you'll put a different type of sprouting seed in each layer of the tower and follow the manufacturer's directions. For a bag setup, simply add seeds, rinse twice a day, and set on top of an absorbent surface like a folded fabric dish towel.

Just like the sprouting lid in the photo on the left, add water to the jar, swirl it around a bit, and drain the excess.

Because they only last a little while, it's best to make smaller quantities and start new batches every few days. Once you see how often you eat sprouts, adjust your growing schedule accordingly.

Warning: Sprouts are fun to watch grow, and they make great science experiments, but children, the elderly, and those who are pregnant or have compromised immune systems are advised by the Food and Drug Administration (FDA) not to eat raw sprouts.

Let's get the safety concerns out of the way. When growing sprouts, you need to ensure that the seeds you buy are expressly made for sprouting. Seeds that you will grow in soil are not inspected and tested for contamination, such as salmonella, like sprouting seeds are. Some regular gardening seeds may even be sprayed with fertilizers to help them grow. When grown to maturity in soil, this isn't a problem, but with sprouts, you're consuming barely-germinated seeds.

Another danger with sprouts is that if you don't follow instructions precisely, the warm, wet environment used to sprout the seeds can become a perfect breeding ground for bacteria and mold. Sprouts are safe for healthy adults when you've followed the instructions. If you see any signs of mold growth or smell anything strange like mustiness or sourness, just throw the sprouts away, sanitize everything, and start again.

Now that I've probably scared you, let's put things into perspective. In 2016, the FDA reported an outbreak of salmonella that covered twelve states. The total number of people who had symptoms was twenty-six, eight were hospitalized, and there were no deaths. The Centers for Disease Control (CDC) estimates an average of 500 deaths in the US as a result of salmonella, and they note that 25% of broiler chickens sold in America are contaminated. So your chances of being harmed by sprouts are quite minimal.

Microgreens

There are two methods for growing microgreens: hydroponically and soil-based. Within those categories, there are variations, but we're going to keep it simple. The most common way to grow microgreens is to use one tray that has holes in it for water drainage. The other method utilizes two solid trays: one to catch excess water below, and the second flipped upside down to cover the seeds until they germinate. We'll call them drainage trays and solid trays to make it easier. They are used for both hydroponic and soil-based methods.

There are many companies that supply great microgreen seeds and equipment, and my two favorites are True Leaf Market and Johnny's Selected Seeds. I talked with True Leaf Market so I could give you the best information on growing microgreens.

Hydroponics Method for Microgreens

With hydroponic microgreen growing, you place the drainage tray into one of the solid trays and lay a microgreen growing mat, a.k.a. a growing pad, on the bottom of the drainage tray. These mats/pads can be made of a variety

Microgreens can be grown in a number of ways. Here they're being grown in a tray.

of materials such as wood pulp, felt, jute, hemp, bamboo, etc. Choose whichever suits you, but look for those called food-safe and biodegradable. The purpose of the mat is to absorb water and to make sure the seeds don't fall into the drainage holes.

My friends at True Leaf Market say to dampen the mat by either spraying it with a water bottle or pouring some water into the solid tray, and then sprinkle the seeds on so that there is space between the seeds equal to about two times the width of the seed. This ensures they're not too crowded and have space to grow. I've overcrowded trays before, and it resulted in a moldy, clumpy mess with *fewer* microgreens rather than more like I had hoped.

Gently mist the seeds with a spray bottle set on the mist setting, then use the spray bottle to moisten the inside second solid tray, flip it over, and place it on top of the seeded drainage tray to act as a blackout humidity dome. Indoor temperatures of between 65°F and 75°F (18°C and 24°C) are perfect for microgreens.

After a few hours, check inside to make sure everything is still moist. Spray again every 8–12 hours as needed, re-covering with the solid cover each time. When the seed leaves (cotyledons) appear after about 3–5 days, wait one more day and then uncover them for good. This is when you'll add about

Grow a variety of microgreens in small containers set inside a basket. It's fun to snip a variety at the dinner table to add a nutrient boost to your salad.

The two-part sprouting tray used in an early section can also be used for microgreens with the addition of a mat. Several varieties of microgreens can be grown in the same tray. (Note: these seeds are a little too close.)

½" (1.3cm) of water to the solid bottom tray. The solid top tray forces the crops to struggle for light, and the bottom watering forces the roots to reach for the water. Counterintuitively, these practices will result in stronger plants, so don't baby them.

Once the dome is removed, it's also time to start giving the plants a lot of light, either natural sunlight or, better yet, grow lights until they're ready to harvest. Check the seed packet to see how long they take—most are ready in about 10 days.

Soil-Based Method for Microgreens

There's not too much difference between the soil-based method and the hydroponic method, but some crops grow better in a soil-based system, like buckwheat, peas, beets, cilantro, and sunflowers.

First, check the seed instructions to see if you should soak them first. Some larger seeds sprout more quickly when soaked, but some seeds don't need soaking at all. Each seed's needs are different, so follow the soaking times carefully, or your seeds may disintegrate.

Put 1½" (3.8cm) of a very light growing medium into a drainage tray and stack it on top of one of the solid trays. The growing medium can be something like the seed starting mix we mentioned earlier, microgreen soil, or even plain coco coir. It needs to be very easy for the seeds to put roots down, but it doesn't need to be super nutritious, because the greens will be growing for a short amount of time.

Dampen the soil with a mister or sprayer, but don't allow it to get soggy. Add seeds thinly, as you would with the hydroponic method, then spray the seeds and cover with a thin layer of additional growing medium. Follow the instructions in the hydroponic method on the previous page regarding the humidity dome and room temperature. You only need to check for moisture and mist these every 12 hours. Then follow the rest of the instructions from the hydroponic method.

Storing Your Microgreens

True Leaf Market says, "Use a colander to rinse your microgreens thoroughly under cold water. Dry the greens completely by spreading over a towel or paper towels and air dry. Speed dry by using a fan on a low setting. Cut greens are best if served right after drying but can be stored loosely

Microgreens come in a wide variety of colors like this spectacular garnet amaranth.

Microgreens like this red kale are packed with nutrients.

Always rinse your microgreens using a colander before consuming.

in a bowl in the refrigerator for several days. Do not try to refrigerate greens that are not completely dry."

Microgreen Kits

I'd seen advertisements for several different microgreen kits on Facebook. I liked the concept of the Hamama Grow Kit, and, at the time, they were offering a free sample kit to the public. I was intrigued, so I contacted the company.

This grow kit from Hamama comes with built-in instructions and easy-to-use seed quilts.

Your microgreens will be ready to eat in no time!

When my kit arrived, I was impressed by the well-thought-out packaging. The outer, recyclable cardboard box perfectly encased the inner package, limiting the amount of excess packing materials. While the growing tray is made of #5 BPA-free plastic, it's reusable and recyclable. The lid is a thin cardboard material, and all the instructions needed to grow your microgreens are printed on the lid. It snugly holds the three seed quilts in the tray.

The instructions are simple: put water into the tray to the fill line, push the seed quilt down until it's saturated, and, in a few days, tear off the top layer. That's it! No need to check the water pH or spray them every day. Seed quilts can be a one-time purchase or part of a subscription plan. As I've said, convenience comes at a cost. As of the printing of this book, the cost of the seed quilts starts at $4.13 with the one-year plan, and a bundle with thirty-six quilts and three reusable growing trays is $149 plus shipping. Remember that this cost is still significantly less than buying them at the market, where a small clamshell container of microgreens is about $5–$10, and the quilt will provide you with at least 2–3 times as much food. You will need to determine if the added ease and benefits are worth the price. I do feel that this is a great, frustration-free kit for children and anyone with very limited mobility.

Baby Greens

There's nothing magical about baby greens—no special equipment or growing practices are needed. These young lettuces and greens are harvested at a stage past microgreens, when they're a few inches (about 7cm) tall, but before they reach full maturity. This results in extra tenderness and sweetness.

You'll get more bang for your buck by growing "cut and come again" seed varieties. Even if they're not listed as "cut and come again," many leaf lettuces and greens will regrow. My philosophy is, you may as well try cutting and see if they grow back, because seeds are cheap compared to buying baby greens in the store. Any variety of leafy lettuces or greens can be harvested at the baby greens stage.

Growing baby greens couldn't be simpler. Because their roots are so small, I like using the same shallow two-part trays I use for growing microgreens, but you can use any shallow container with adequate

GROWING MICROGREENS FOR PROFIT

Maybe a side business in microgreens could be in your future, too.

Larry Hountz, from City-Hydro, makes over $100,000 per year growing microgreens in his small rowhome in Baltimore, Maryland, only spending about $100 a month on electricity and using just 7 gallons (26.5L) of water per day.

Best of all, he teaches others how to do it. I appreciate that he has free, open-source training in addition to offering private training and products. He advises that people talk to restaurant owners and look at local farmer's markets to assess needs and interest *before* purchasing all the equipment. You can grow microgreens all day long, but if you don't have a place to sell them, you're just wasting money.

Although I haven't used them personally, City-Hydro systems seem to be high quality, with food-safe plastics, sturdy shelves, custom-made grow lights, and good growing mats. Instead of regular flimsy nursery flats, like the ones used in seed starting (see Chapter 12), Larry uses heavy-duty 24" x 16" (61 x 40.5cm) pizza dough proofing pans, which will last a lifetime. He sells full trays of microgreens for around $30 and half trays for about $20. Smaller containers for sale at farmer's markets go for $5–$10. Larry has taught more than 5,000 people around the world how to grow and sell microgreens successfully. Check out his YouTube channel, Larry Hountz.

drainage. Fill it with a good seed starting mix to within ½" (1.3cm) of the top of the tray or container and moisten well. The seeds actually germinate better with fewer nutrients, so using a rich potting mix or just compost is not as good. You will add fertilizer later. Seed starting mix is also lighter, making it easier for delicate lettuce roots to push through.

After seeding lightly, not as thickly as you would with microgreens, put an additional ¼" (0.6cm) of moistened seed starting mix on top and gently pat so the seeds come in contact with the mix. Place a clear plastic dome over the tray or cover lightly with plastic food wrap. Remove the dome or plastic wrap as soon as you start seeing green.

When plants break the ground, the first pair of leaves you see are the cotyledons, which look different than the second and subsequent leaves, which are called the true leaves. Once you see the true leaves, you can feed your lettuce a diluted (half strength) liquid fertilizer high in nitrogen for good leaf development. When the plants are about 2"–4" (5–10cm) tall, you can harvest the tender leaves by cutting them with a clean, sharp knife or scissors, leaving at least 1" (2.5cm) of plant material above the ground. From here, they will usually regrow. You should get around three or four harvests per planting, although the more you cut, the slower they may regrow and the sparser the subsequent harvests.

This mixture of green and red lettuces will make a lovely addition to your dinner plate.

PART 4

WHAT TO GROW

In this part of the book, we'll discuss planning what to grow based on the method(s) you've chosen, variety selection, and how much to grow. The plant profiles in Chapter 11 will help you learn the basics of growing several different common indoor gardening crops. We'll even talk about seed starting and seed saving.

This section will be most helpful to those of you with little gardening experience, but even you expert gardeners will find useful information here, especially if this is your first venture into the world of indoor gardening.

Many seed companies offer smaller
varieties of different crops that
are perfect for indoor gardening,
like this Tom Thumb Snow Pea.

CHAPTER 10

Planning and Growing

Is there anything more exciting than when your crops start poking their heads out of the soil like this garlic? Planning when and how to grow each crop is how you can get to this point.

Before you actually put the first seeds into the soil, you'll need to understand the plants you're choosing to grow. Look ahead on their grow schedule, understand the process by which they'll grow, and in general have a plan for how your garden will unfold. In this chapter, we'll briefly touch upon these factors as well as introduce you to choosing between varieties of a single plant. Then, in Chapter 11, we'll truly dive into the specific plant profiles.

How Long Do Plants Last?

Plants don't last forever. You'll want to know if the plants you're growing are annuals or perennials—like this horseradish, which is a perennial and grows for several years.

When I teach veggie gardening, one of the most common questions I get is, "Why did my plant die?" If you're a beginner gardener, you might not know it, but different plants have different life cycles. Also, *all* plants will eventually die. The three life cycles of your plants can be annual, biennial, and perennial.

Annual plants: These only live for a short time—a single growing season. If you want fresh lettuce throughout the year, you should plant maybe three or four leaf lettuce plants continually, about every other week. As they grow, you can cut a couple outer leaves off of each plant for your salad and let the center continue to grow until it becomes bitter. Then remove the whole plant. From seed to removal takes an average of seven weeks, depending on which variety you grow. That's the typical lifespan of lettuce; radishes live for about four weeks, and broccoli for about sixteen weeks. It's always best to pick things as soon as they are ripe—the younger, the better. Other examples of annual plants are basil, cilantro, cucumbers, beans, and peas. Look online for each of your crops to learn how to tell when they're ready to harvest and how to properly pick and store them. If you plan to save seeds for next year, choose one plant that you let go to seed. Plants have different ways they seed, but let's look at leaf lettuces as an example. You'll know that the plant is past its prime when you notice that the lettuce starts to taste bitter. Soon the center of the plant will start to grow tall, and several tall stalks will appear to grow out of the center of the plant. Eventually, you'll see buds emerge from the stalks, then small white or yellow flowers, which will turn into fluffy "down" (think of the way dandelions go from the yellow flowers to the white puff, but not as full). The lettuce seeds will form, and you can collect the seeds when the flower heads look dry. There will be plenty, so don't be afraid to remove a flower head, open it up, and see if the seeds are dry. Each plant's seeds need to be collected in a different way. A great resource to learn how to harvest and save seeds is Seed Savers Exchange (*www.SeedSavers.org*).

Biennial plants: Carrots are an example of a biennial plant; biennial means the plant can be eaten the first year, but they don't produce seeds until the second year. If you want to eat the carrot, do so as soon as it's ready to harvest. However, if you want to collect seeds, allow one carrot to keep growing into the second year when it will flower and produce seeds. Other edible biennial crops include parsley, fennel, some cabbages, and members of the onion family, like leeks.

Perennial plants: These plants live and bear for several years, but even they don't last forever. A great example of a perennial plant is the herb mint. The plant produces beautiful leaves for several months, then it may start to look bad and even lose all its leaves. The stems may become hard, and the plant will look dead. But if you prune it, and keep it slightly moist, it will eventually come back to life. Watercress is an easy-to-grow perennial. Strawberries send out side shoots that will bury themselves in the soil and form new plants, which can then be cut from the "mother" plant. Other examples of edible perennials are plants that grow from rhizomes like ginger, horseradish, and turmeric. Look online to learn more about how to care for each perennial crop.

So, just remember—you can do everything right, and your plant will eventually die. It's just a matter of when.

What Variety Should I Grow?

Think of how you want to use your crop before selecting the variety. The fruit of this Inca Jewel tomato will all be ready at about the same time, which makes it perfect for making sauce.

Before we talk about varieties of different crops, I want to reiterate that, without using supplemental lighting, you'll only be successful with plants that don't require a lot of light—those that grow in so-called partial shade where the plants receive less than six hours of direct light a day, or longer periods of dappled sun where the sun is filtered through tree leaves outside the windows. These will be your "cool season" crops like leaf lettuces, greens, quick-growing root veggies, and some of your brassicas, which are members of the cabbage/broccoli family. Note that they may take longer to mature than crops grown outdoors in sunnier locations or when using grow lights.

If you've ever looked at a seed catalog or an online seed store, you've noticed how many different types of each vegetable there are. Although you'll most commonly see the word *variety* used in seed catalogs, you may occasionally run across the word *cultivar* as well, which stands for cultivated variety. Although the words are often interchanged, a variety is defined as a grouping of a species that's found in nature, while a cultivar has usually had some human intervention to produce it. All varieties and cultivars are members of the same species and can interbreed. In the scientific naming, variety names come after the word "var.", and cultivars come at the end in single quotation marks. For example, *Brassica oleracea* var. *italica* is your common broccoli variety, and *Cucumis sativusis* 'Muncher' is a specific cultivar of cucumber. Cultivar names are often quite colorful, descriptive, or even strange, whereas variety names tend to seem more scientific. Given the common use of the word "variety" to include cultivars in gardening writing and its non-gardening general definition of "type," I will continue to use the word "variety" to refer to either varieties or cultivars, as the distinction will not matter to the casual home gardener.

What should you look for when choosing a specific variety of veggie? First, decide how you intend to use it or what part of the plant you'll be eating. Next, see which variety grows quickest, especially if it's for indoor growing. Even with good lighting, you may experience slower growth than if you were growing the same crops outside. Then, research what varieties might be heavy producers, so you get more yield per plant. If you've had problems in the past, look for varieties that are more pest- or disease-resistant. Even though pest and disease problems don't happen as frequently as when plants are grown outdoors, they can still be a problem, especially with those pests and diseases that commonly plague houseplants.

You can also select cultivars based on their cool factor or uniqueness. For instance, why grow plain old Swiss chard when you can grow a variety called Oriole Orange that has bright orange stems? I live near Baltimore, so the Orioles are my baseball team, and their colors are orange and black, making this the perfect variety for me. Outside, one of my favorite things to grow is the Anne Arundel Muskmelon. I chose that variety because I live in Anne Arundel County, Maryland, and it's been grown in my county since around 1731. It has history.

Let's look at some examples of different common indoor food plant varieties and what makes them distinct from one another.

Cultivar names, like this Swiss chard type called Oriole Orange, are often quite helpfully descriptive.

Beets

Cheltenham Green Top

Although you can eat both the roots and greens of most beet varieties, if you're not particularly fond of beetroots, then you'll want to look for varieties with the tastiest leaves. I like Ruby Queen for beetroots because they are quick-growing (about 55 days) and have a mild, sweet flavor. They are also smaller in size, which makes them great for roasting or canning.

Cheltenham Green Top beets grow long and tapered—reminiscent of a carrot. While the roots are quite tasty, I enjoy the greens steamed or chopped fresh in a salad. Another option if you just want the leaves is to grow beet's cousin, Swiss chard, which does not form bulbs and which has great-tasting leaves reminiscent of beet greens.

By the way, although you can eat sugar beets, they aren't very tasty. If you do try them, I'd suggest roasting them. They'll be pretty sweet, so combine them with other, less sweet root veggies to balance the flavors.

Ruby Queen

Carrots

Have you ever bought a bunch of carrots at the store, planning on turning them into a nice glass of juice? You get home, take out your expensive juicer, scrub the carrots, and cut them into big chunks. They look gorgeous—a good, solid orange with a nice flavor when you pop one of the chunks into your mouth. You turn on the juicer, load in the carrot chunks, and the only thing that comes out is a little dribble.

Let me guess—those carrots were fat at the top and tapered to a thin point at the other end, right? I hate to be the bearer of bad news, but that variety of carrot is for eating, not juicing. Juicing carrots will usually be more cylindrical and have a stubbier, blunt end. In general, they are sweeter and absorb more water than regular eating carrots. More than likely, they are from the Nantes variety.

The great thing about Nantes carrots is that they tend to grow faster than other types of carrots, and they're also delicious when eaten raw or cooked. You can use a juicing carrot for eating, but you cannot expect good juice from an eating carrot. Juicing carrots are hard to find in the store, so they're a great choice to grow at home.

Danvers Half-Long

Because of my background using and teaching the Square Foot Gardening method, with its shorter raised beds, I got in the habit of growing shorter carrots. But Danvers Half-Longs are still my choice for eating carrots because they fit well in containers. If I could only grow one variety of carrot, however, it would be Koral because of its sweet and crisp flesh. They're great for eating raw or cooked, and are even better for juicing.

Koral

Cucumbers

The two main categories of cucumbers are pickling and slicing. Slicing "cukes" are usually peeled and eaten fresh, while pickling cukes often have thinner skin and are processed or pickled.

Muncher cucumbers can easily be grown in a container just 12" (30.5cm) wide. They're a great choice for fresh eating with tender flesh that is not bitter. Another great feature is that they're quite disease-resistant.

Monika is an especially good variety for indoor growing for many reasons. These quick-growing beauties are great for both pickling and slicing. Best of all, they don't need pollination, which makes them an exceptional choice for an indoor garden.

Both varieties need a vertical structure to climb on; they must be in a south-facing window and may even need supplemental lighting, either full-spectrum or red.

When choosing slicing cucumbers, you may have seen varieties that are called "burpless." In fact, many cucumbers seem to cause digestive issues, such as burping and flatulence, in some people who eat them. Burpless

Muncher

cucumbers ostensibly reduce or eliminate this unpleasant reaction. There doesn't seem to be a true burp-free cucumber, but English varieties seem to result in less burping than others.

While cooked cucumbers aren't a staple for Americans, they are quite common in many other countries, especially amongst Asian cultures. Try a few in your next stir-fry.

Monika

Tomatoes

The most important factor in choosing a tomato variety is how you plan to use it. Do you want a tomato for fresh eating? Then you'll probably want an indeterminate variety where one or two tomatoes ripen at a time so it's ready for your salad. Indeterminate varieties usually grow on a vine with the bottom tomatoes ripening first and the ripening progressively moving up the vine during the season. Because vining varieties require a trellis or other tall support structure, I mainly recommend sticking with tomato varieties labeled "container," "dwarf," or "micro-dwarf."

Determinate tomatoes are usually bush varieties, and all of the tomatoes ripen within a few days. This is the type to grow if you want a lot of tomatoes to be ready at once so you can make a batch of pasta sauce or salsa. They are usually meatier, with thicker walls, fewer seeds, and less juice.

When growing tomatoes indoors, whether determinate or indeterminate, look for varieties that grow quickly. They are usually intended for those living in the northern United States, where there's a shorter growing season. We'll talk about "Days to Maturity" later in this chapter, but tomato cultivars vary widely and can take anywhere from about 50 days to more than 100 days to mature.

In the last few years, I've become enthralled by the number of new dwarf varieties being introduced by the Dwarf Tomatoes Project, run by Craig LeHoullier, author of the book *Epic Tomatoes*. These plants have been

Martino's Roma

painstakingly bred to produce luscious, full-size eating tomatoes on a small plant—perfect for indoor growing with supplemental lighting.

Craig notes that there are many factors to consider with tomatoes: flavor profile (mild to intense and sweet to tart), color, plant size (micros, dwarfs, or full-size), etc. Indoors and out, I try a couple new varieties each year.

Martino's Roma tomato is a great multi-use selection if you only have room for one tomato. This dwarf-determinate variety is great for salsa and cooking but is also pleasant for fresh eating. Tomato Micro Tom is a nice dwarf hybrid indeterminate variety that's great if you're growing indoors but don't have enough space for a full-sized tomato, since it only grows about 6"–8" (15–20cm) tall. It's a great choice for a small container and even fits on a windowsill.

Micro Tom

But How Should I Decide What to Grow?

First off, think about what you and your family like and you know they will eat. My suggestion, when trying any new form of gardening, is to start small! Initially, limit your growing methods to one or two. If this is your first time gardening, limit your crop choices to no more than six. You'll need to learn the basics of gardening *and* indoor gardening at the same time. Starting too big or growing too many different things at the same time can easily cause you to become overwhelmed. When you get overwhelmed, you can become discouraged and may abandon gardening altogether. The great thing about indoor gardening is that you won't have to wait for a whole new growing year to expand your garden if you like.

So, start by making a wish list of what you want to grow. Do you have enough space and resources to grow everything on your list? For instance, if you want to grow a ton of fruiting veggies like tomatoes, peppers, and eggplants, will you have enough heat mats and grow lights to accomplish that? If not, maybe you should start with just a couple of dwarf or micro-dwarf plants that can be covered by a single light.

Are you growing in a small space? Then make the best use of your space by growing the food that will give you the biggest return on investment or the biggest sense of pride or adventure. Herbs and tender gourmet lettuces make more sense to me than something like potatoes, which are readily available at the grocery store year-round at a reasonable price. Now, if you love a unique variety of potato not available in the store and just *have* to have it, that would be a completely different story. If there's something you'd like to experiment with, and you have the time, space, and resources to do so, by all means, do it.

Next, look at the method(s) you're using, and figure out what are the best crops to grow using which method. Other than a small plug-and-play system, hydroponics was fairly new to me before I wrote this book. The system I'm using lends itself to growing leafy greens and lettuces, but not things like root vegetables, so I know to stick with what will grow in it. But that doesn't mean I'm stuck growing thirty-six of the same thing.

Remember: some crops like it cooler while others thrive in the heat. When growing indoors, I divide my plant list

When deciding what to grow, you'll need to consider your space limitations, what will or won't grow indoors well, and what crops will give you the biggest monetary return.

into cool-season and warm-season veggies and plan the best location for their needs. Most of the cool-, part shade–loving plants I put upstairs on a desk in the guest room where they get afternoon sun with a dose of supplemental lighting. Those with more moderate needs, I put in the office. Heat-loving, fruiting crops, I grow in containers that I place on top of a heat mat with plenty of supplemental lighting that have the red spectrum light they need to flower and fruit.

It may seem like a never-ending process to decide what to plant. Take a deep breath and remember: the more planning you do at the kitchen table, the less physical work you'll need to do and re-do, and the less money you'll waste on things you don't need. By considering all these factors and by drawing out a few lists and cross-referencing them, you will be able to figure out a list of crops you want to and can grow. You can do this any way you choose to, including by general note-taking and journaling (see page 106), but if you want, try the What Will I Grow? Worksheet on page 112!

Once you've gotten started with your indoor gardening journey and had your first successful (or not) harvest, don't forget to try a new crop. Every year, I try to grow one or two things that are new to me so that I can expand my plant-growing knowledge—and my palate. Even if you want to stick with the same crops, try a different variety of the crop. My new crop last year was New Zealand spinach, which isn't a true spinach at all. When I spoke with Renee Shepherd of Renee's Garden Seeds, she told me that it tastes much better cooked than raw. She was right. It will definitely be on my list again, since it was easier to grow than a true spinach. Yes, even though I've been gardening for decades, I still make lists of what to grow. And my new variety for this year? I'm trying two new micro tomatoes—Micro Tom and Orange Hat from Baker Creek Seeds.

Journaling

Once you've decided what to grow, if you don't already do this, I'd like to introduce you to garden journaling. Grab a journal or a spiral notebook, or open your laptop and journal digitally. I prefer journaling digitally or using a three-ring binder with lined notebook paper, since I like to put my crops in alphabetical order, and I'm able to move the information in a digital document or physically move the pages in the binder.

Write down every variety of every crop you want to grow, then go to an online seed selling site to see how to grow them (or get started from the Plant Profiles in Chapter 11). Can you start seeds ahead of time in trays, or is it better to direct sow? How far apart should you plant them? How much light do they need? Are they a cool- or warm-weather crop? How long do they take to grow? See the next page for information on Days to Maturity (DTM) and Days to Harvest (DTH).

Important: If it's not listed on the site with the seed information, separately research what pests and diseases might affect that particular plant.

Use a separate page for each crop you intend to grow and write down all the info you've found. You can make your own How to Grow section and list things like light

and water requirements, how deep to plant the seeds, the height and width of the mature plants, etc.

After you start your garden, you can note where and when you got the seeds, and journal about how long it took to grow, if you had any pest or disease problems, how you handled the problem, and note if you want to grow this particular variety again, or if you'd like to try another instead. You can include as much or as little information as you'd like. The point is to get the information down so you aren't constantly looking up the same information or trying to remember whether something worked last time.

Though it's somewhat limited in scope, the worksheet on page 112 is a great starting point to synthesize the basic info about what you want as well as what you are capable of doing. Start there and then compile more detailed notes about specific seeds before purchasing them.

Herbs and Spices

By far, you will get the biggest return on investment by growing herbs and spices indoors. Look at any article on the most profitable garden crops, and you'll likely see herbs and spices. In addition to growing these to flavor your favorite food dishes, many herbs and spices can be used medicinally and to make wonderful herbal teas.

What is the difference between an herb and a spice? This is a hard question to answer and can be the source of heated discussion. Some sources say that if the primary part of the plant used is its leaves, it's an herb, and a spice refers to other

Journaling, whether in a physical book or in digital documents and spreadsheets, will help you keep track of your desires and your results.

If you grow herbs close together, be sure you constantly harvest the leaves. Having the same care needs is a bonus, but this sage won't be in the container as long as the rosemary and thyme, so it doesn't matter.

parts of the plant, such as the bark, seeds, or roots. Another definition is that an herb is the fresh leaves, seeds, and flowers used as a flavoring for food that is not the main part of the dish, whereas spices are dried, may also contain the roots and bark, and are also used as flavoring and not the main part of the dish.

Neither of these definitions is completely accurate. I tend to favor the first definition about the leaves being an herb and the rest of the plant being a spice. To me, things like oregano, thyme, and basil, grown for their leaves, should be considered herbs, but the second definition would consider them as spices when the same leaves have been dried. We're not even going to address the botanical definition, since a banana tree is technically an herb, and things we call spices like cumin, turmeric, and cardamom come from plants that are botanically herbs.

And, please, don't get me started on garlic, which is technically a vegetable even though it's not the main part of a dish and can be used either fresh or dried.

Whatever you choose to call them, these healthy flavor powerhouses are usually simple to grow, don't require the best soil, and don't mind a little neglect. Most of them are also a great option if you don't have a lot of light available.

How Much Should I Grow?

Now, take that list of all the vegetables and herbs you've decided to grow and note how much of each you and your family eat weekly or monthly. For instance, my husband and I eat an average of two heads of Romaine lettuce a week, so it makes sense for me to start at least two new lettuce plants each week. I can start them in seed trays so I can more closely monitor them. We might only go through twelve radishes a month, though, so I'll direct sow a couple radishes throughout my indoor garden every month, since they tend to be ready to harvest at different times. Unlike outdoor gardening, the beauty of growing indoors is that you'll be able to grow year-round with supplemental lighting. If you're depending solely on window light, your crop selection and timing options will be limited, but with proper planning, you'll still get a great harvest.

How Long Will it Take?

Look at your seed packets or the label on your transplant, and you might see the letters DTM (days to maturity) or DTH (days to harvest). If the information is not on the plant label, look at an online seed seller's website for that information. You'll need to do this for every different variety of every single crop you intend to grow. As we covered earlier, this is necessary because your chosen variety may take a lot longer, or a lot shorter, than the average figure you usually get in a magazine article.

Both DTM and DTH tell you approximately when you can expect to be able to harvest from your plant. Knowing this information will help you be able to plan for having room to start more plants for a year-round harvest, if that's your goal. If you're depending on

It's all well and good to have a successful indoor garden, but be careful not to bite off more than you can chew—you may need to give away extra crops if your appetite can't keep up with your plants.

Planning your gardening based on each plant's growing schedule will help you anticipate when you can expect to enjoy the results of your hard labor.

transplants from the garden center, obviously you're subject to their seasonal availability. However, if you've got a little extra room, starting your own seeds so that you're ready to fill an empty space is a great strategy. It just takes a little more planning. See Chapter 12 for information on seed starting.

So, what's the difference between DTM and DTH? It depends on who you ask. I couldn't find a consistent answer in my research, and, horticulturally, there doesn't seem to be a real difference between the two. So, I went directly to the expert, Renee Shepherd of Renee's Garden Seeds; her answer seems to be the most common, and it's the one I've used for years. On her company's seed packets, the DTM measures the time from when you transplant a seedling that you started ahead of time to when you harvest from the plant. For direct seeded (a.k.a. direct sown) crops, the DTH measures the time from the day you plant the seed in the soil to when you harvest from the plant. Direct sown crops are those plants that don't do well when started in a seed tray and then moved to a container or outdoors into the ground. Since we're growing indoors, you can direct sow any of your crops. So, if you see DTM, but you plan to direct sow the seeds into their final location instead of transplanting, you'll need to tack on about 4–6 weeks to get your functional DTH.

To summarize, both DTM and DTH give you the expected time you will be able to harvest from the plant but measured from two distinct points in a plant's life:

- **DTM** = Days To Maturity, measured from the day the transplant/seedling goes to its final growing location
- **DTH** = Days To Harvest, measured from the day the seed goes into the soil for direct sown crops

If we look at Renee's Garden Seeds website for a container lettuce, as an example, there's a variety called Ruby & Emerald Duet. The information says to direct sow and gives you a lot of growing hints like thinning, final spacing, watering, fertilizing, etc. The Days to Harvest is 50–67 days. Why such a large DTH range? Because there are several factors that go into growing, including sun exposure, temperature, etc., even when you're growing indoors. It's not clockwork!

The Birds and the Bees: Pollination

Do you intend to grow anything that depends on pollinators like bees, birds, or moths to produce fruits? Do you know which vegetables and fruits those are, and how to deal with the lack of pollinators?

Generally speaking, if a plant flowers and the main part that's eaten are the fruits, they should be pollinated. This includes things like tomatoes, eggplants, tomatillos, cucumbers, and strawberries. (If you're growing corn, even though the main part you're eating are the seeds, you would need to hand-pollinate that, too. I don't recommend growing corn indoors, though.)

Other crops that flower but are eaten for the seed, like peas and beans, do not need to be pollinated. Plants eaten for the roots, like radishes and carrots, or those eaten for their leaves, such as lettuce and greens, do not require pollination either. Other plants that do not need pollination are members of the brassica family: cabbages, kale, etc.

Let's dive a little deeper into how pollination actually works before learning how you can achieve the pollination you need.

There are two basic types of pollination—self-pollination and cross-pollination. In general terms, self-pollination means you're dealing with one plant, while cross-pollination means you're dealing with two or more plants.

I'm going to introduce you now to three scientific terms, but I don't want you to get hung up on trying to remember the names. You just need to know the basic concept of these three to help you understand how you'll need to get a bigger harvest from your crops.

Autogamy is a form of self-pollination where you have a single plant and all the action takes place within a single flower on that one plant. The pollen doesn't have to be transferred from one flower to another. You may have heard the term "perfect flower," which means that the blossom has both male and female parts. Tomato blossoms are an example of autogamous blossoms. Once pollinated, you'll see a small tomato form in the middle of the blossom.

- What to remember: one plant, one flower = pollination
- Example: tomatoes, peppers, and eggplants

Geitonogamy is another type of self-pollination where the pollen grains from the anther (male part) transfer to

These "perfect flower" plants (tomato, pepper, and eggplant) don't need your help to pollinate because the male and female parts are within each single blossom, but you can encourage strong fruiting by helping them anyway.

the stigma (female part) between different flowers that are on the same plant. Note: While tomatoes, peppers, and eggplants *can* pollinate with one flower (as listed above), I feel they pollinate better when transferring pollen from flower to flower.

- What to remember: one plant, two flowers = pollination
- Example: corn, cucumbers

Xenogamy is a type of cross-pollination that involves the transfer of pollen that takes place from the flowers of two different plants. When reading a fruit tree catalog, you'll sometimes see that you must plant two bushes or trees in order to ensure pollination.

- What to remember: two plants, two flowers = pollination
- Example: blueberries, kiwis, and other fruit varieties that are not listed as self-pollinating

When grown outdoors, the wind, birds, bees, and other insects would take care of any necessary pollination. Basically, anything that causes pollen to dislodge from the male parts of a blossom and land on the female parts can cause pollination. But you will need to hand-pollinate certain plants when growing indoors. Even if your crops are self-pollinating, to maximize your harvest, you will want to help the pollination process along. Although a fan may do the job similarly the way wind would work outside, you will get a noticeably larger harvest if you make a personal effort to pollinate. Following are a couple simple ways to pollinate.

Take the job of pollination seriously if you want to enjoy the fruits of your labor!

Shake Method

Self-pollinating crops might just need a little shake of the plant by hand to dislodge the pollen. Some gardeners swear that using an old battery-powered toothbrush to cause the shaking gives them even better pollination. It certainly can't hurt, and it seems logical that the vibration might do the job a little better. Try it if you want!

Manual Transfer Method

Another option for self-pollinating plants is manual pollination. Although it's optional for "perfect flower" plants (those autogamous plants with male and female parts within a single flower), manual pollination will be a must for geitonogamous crops with separate male and female blossoms (and, of course, for xenogamous multiple plants too). It's simple to do with something like a small artist paintbrush with soft bristles or even a cotton swab.

For plants like these, including cucumbers, first you identify the male and female blossoms (on the single plant). Usually a long, straight stem holds the male blossom, while a tiny, unpollinated fruit holds the female blossom. As soon as you see the female blossom open up, it's time to pollinate—don't wait, as female blossoms may fade quickly and die.

The flower petals serve as a protective covering for the reproductive parts, but all the action takes place in the very center of the blossoms. Take the brush or swab and gently but thoroughly twirl it in the center of the male blossom, then transfer the pollen to the middle of the female blossom and brush well. For more thorough pollination, go back and forth from several male blossoms and fertilize several females. Think of how a bee flits from flower to flower.

Pollinating with pollen from several male flowers, as well as pollinating a female flower a few days in a row, may help prevent what is called incomplete pollination. When a plant isn't well pollinated, it can result in fewer or misshapen fruits being produced.

Certain plants, such as eggplant and this cucumber, will need your manual help getting pollinated if you want to enjoy their fruits. You can do this with a paintbrush or cotton swab.

Manual Blossom Removal Method

Another way to pollinate if you don't want to use a brush or swab is to remove the male blossom from the plant, remove the petals, and use this to pollinate a female blossom.

This photo shows the removing blossom method on a squash blossom outdoors, but it is a good representation of what you would do.

With plants like cucumbers and squash, the male blossom has a thin stem behind the blossom (top), whereas the female has an immature fruit behind the blossom (bottom).

CROSS-VARIETY POLLINATION

You may have heard that you shouldn't plant cucumbers next to melons because they are both from the same plant family (Cucumis) or that if you plant sweet peppers next to hot peppers, it will change their flavors because of cross-pollination. That's simply not true for the current season's crops, but it could definitely affect next year's crops if you plan on saving seeds and they were to cross-pollinate. Learn more about saving seeds in Chapter 12 to decide if this is going to be a consideration for you.

Here is a handy worksheet you can use to get all your ideas and notes down on paper. I filled out a realistic sample to give you an idea of how it works. If this kind of structure doesn't work for you, feel free to organize your notes however you see fit.

Crops wish list	Light needs: full sun (FS), part shade (PS), supplemental light (SUP)	Water needs: low, med., high	Possible varieties/uses	Where to buy	Where to grow/notes
1. Carrots	PS	Medium	Juicing (Nantes?)	Renee's Garden	Spare room with grow lights?
2. Lettuce	PS	Medium	Many varieties	Baker Creek	Spare room and hydroponic in office
3. Tomatoes	FS SUP	High	Dwarf Cherry	Click and Grow (pod)	Kitchen under cabinets (built-in grow light)
4. Peppers	FS SUP	High	Dwarf Hot	Click and Grow (pod)	Kitchen under cabinets (built-in grow light)
5. Basil	FS SUP	High	Common	Click and Grow (pod)	Kitchen under cabinets (built-in grow light)
6. Cucumbers	FS SUP	High	Whatever I can order online easily	Not sure yet	Kitchen under cabinets (built-in grow light)
7. Swiss Chard			Oriole Orange	Baker Creek	Garden tower (office)
8. Rosemary & Thyme	FS SUP	Low	Any	Renee's Garden	Pot in office/sandy soil or kitchen window
9. Peas	FS SUP	High	Little Crunch	Renee's Garden	Pot in office/short cage, trellis
10. Microgreens	PS	Medium	Mixed	True Leaf Market Hawama	Table in kitchen

Possible rooms/locations	Description	Methods/notes
1. Basement	Pretty cold and dark, would need grow lights and heating	Grow tent-shelves, soil-based containers, lighting, ventilation. (?) heater OR hydroponic with lighting and heat
2. Office	Gets a lot of direct sunlight year-round	NFT hydroponic, shoe tower, Garden Tower 2, wall pocket
3. Kitchen, under cabinets	Has undercabinet lighting	PS or shade crops only—put plants close to the light, small plug-and-play hydroponic system w/grow light
4. Kitchen, windowsill	Is south-facing, gets a lot of sunlight	Soil-based pots/turn pots weekly, move pots (front to back)
5. Spare bedroom	Has north-facing windows, so low light; on second floor, so weight is a concern	NFT hydroponic or soil-based. MUST have really good supplemental lighting or use a plug-and-play system with integrated grow lights

Crops wish list	Light needs: full sun (FS), part shade (PS), supplemental light (SUP)	Water needs: low, med., high	Possible varieties/uses	Where to buy	Where to grow/notes

Possible rooms/locations	Description	Methods/notes

CHAPTER 11

Plant Profiles

Be adventurous with your
veggie and herb selections.

In this chapter, we'll cover general information about common and delicious plants to help you grow your crops. Each plant has its own dedicated section. Check the seed packets or an online seed seller for more detailed information, since different varieties tend to have different needs—the information here should be a guideline to get you started only. When I recommend a number of plants, it's usually for two people based on one serving a week, so scale up or down as needed based on family size and how much you eat of each veggie.

Remember to be strategic! Use the light information to group your crops together. For instance, put your beets and beans near each other closest to a south-facing window or where they're sharing grow lights for the same number of hours per day. Your greens and lettuces can share space where the lighting is not as strong. Tomatoes, peppers, and other fruiting crops will need strong window light plus supplemental lighting, either full-spectrum or dedicated red lighting for bloom and fruit production. See Chapter 4 for more information about supplemental lighting.

At-a-Glance Plants Chart

To get you started, this chapter kicks off with several pages that break down the absolute essentials about a selection of the most popular featured plants. Not every plant in this chapter is featured in the chart—rather, the chart is meant to be an easy, accessible jumping-off point where you can quickly compare some of the most likely options for your home garden and see their different needs. Feel free to skim it, refer back to it, circle or highlight it—whatever is useful to you! But don't forget to delve into the full plant profiles in this chapter so that you don't miss out on any of the less common plants that might be of interest to you.

Also included in this At-a-Glance Plants Chart is a **special section on fruits**. With the exception of strawberries, which have their own dedicated plant profile, the fruits featured in the chart are not profiled in this book in additional detail. That is because they are multi-year investments, are often more sensitive to climate and light, require partial time outdoors on a deck or patio, and are overall more challenging to grow to fruition. That said, if you are up to the challenge and the time commitment, I want to encourage you to give one of them a try!

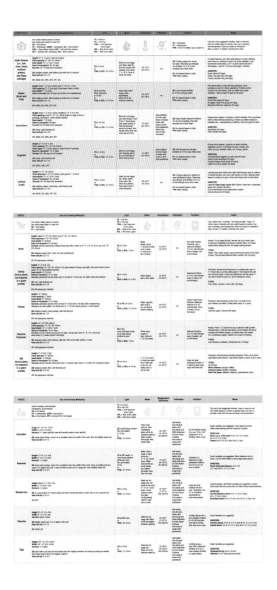

VEGETABLES	Info and Growing Method(s)	Light	Water
	Info varies widely based on variety See online seed seller for best info **SB** = Soil-Based **HY** = Hydroponic (**AERO** = Aeroponics; **DS** = Drip System; **DWC** = Deep Water Culture; **EFS** = Ebb and Flow System; **NFT** = Nutrient Film Technique; **WS** = Wick System)	**FS** = Full Sun **PS** = Part Sun **FSGL** = Full-Spectrum Grow Lights **BGL** = Blue Grow Lights **RGL** = Red Grow Lights	
Asian Greens (i.e., bok choy, tatsoi, mustard greens; also Napa cabbage)	**Height:** 3"–2' (7.5cm–0.6m) and higher **Plant spacing:** 6"–24" (15–60cm) **Seed depth:** ¼"–½" (0.6–1.3cm) **Seed to transplant:** 30–40 days **Harvest:** 40–70 days from transplant **SB:** shallow-rooted; well-draining soil with lots of compost **Best soil pH:** 6.0–7.0 **HY:** AERO, DS, DWC, EFS, NFT, WS	**PS:** 6–8 hrs or **FSGL or BGL:** 10–12 hrs	Moist but not soggy soil. Water daily for first two weeks after planting, then about 1"–2" (2.5–5cm) of water per week
Beans (Bush and Pole)	**Height:** bush 1'–2' (0.3–0.6m); pole 7'–15' (2.1–4.6m) **Plant spacing:** 3" (7.5cm) apart (pole beans need a trellis) **Seed depth:** 1" (2.5cm) **Seed to harvest:** 50–60 days (do not like to be transplanted) **SB:** shallow-rooted; well-draining soil with lots of compost **Best soil pH:** 6.0–7.0 **HY:** AERO, DS, DWC, NFT, WS	**FS** in morning **PS** in afternoon 8–10 hrs or **FSGL or BGL:** 12–16 hrs	Keep moist when young. After established, allow soil to dry between watering
Cucumbers	**Height:** bush 1'–2' (0.3–0.6m); climbing 6'–8' (1.8–2.4m) **Plant spacing:** bush 6"–12" (15–30cm) (stake or cage at time of planting); climbing 6" (15cm) (trellis needed) **Seed depth:** 1" (2.5cm) **Seed to transplant:** 20 days **Harvest:** 50–70 days from transplant **SB:** loose, well-draining soil **Best soil pH:** 6.0–6.5 **HY:** AERO, DS, DWC, EFS, NFT	**FS:** 8–10 hrs or **FSGL or RGL:** 12–16 hrs	Moist but not soggy soil. Stick finger in soil. If dry 2" (5cm) down, then water slowly so that soil becomes evenly saturated. Mist leaves every other day when the air is dry
Eggplant	**Height:** 2'–4' (0.6–1.2m) **Plant spacing:** 18"–24" (45–60cm) **Seed depth:** ½" (1.3cm) (stake or cage at time of planting) **Seed to transplant:** 14–21 days **Harvest:** 65–80 days from transplant **SB:** loose, well-draining soil **Best soil pH:** 6.0–7.0 **HY:** AERO, DWC, NFT	**FS:** 8–10 hrs or **FSGL or RGL:** 12–16 hrs	Moist but not soggy soil. Allowing soil to dry out will result in bitter-tasting fruits
Lettuce (Leaf)	**Height:** 4"–8" (10–20cm) **Plant spacing:** 6"–8" (15–20cm); baby greens 1" (2.5cm) **Seed depth:** ¼"–½" (0.6–1.3cm) **Seed to transplant:** 20–30 days **Harvest:** 45–55 days from transplant **SB:** shallow-rooted; likes loose, well-draining soil **Best soil pH:** 6.0–6.5 **HY:** AERO, DS, DWC, NFT, WS	**PS:** 8–10 hrs or **FSGL or BGL:** 10–12 hrs	Moist but not soggy soil. Water lightly every other day when first planted, then about twice a week thereafter

Temperature	Pollination	Fertilizer	Notes
(thermometer icon)	(flower icon)	**SB** = Soil-Based **HY** = Hydroponics **PPM** = Parts Per Million (see Chapter 8)	Tips and a few suggested varieties. Days to maturity will vary wildly based on variety, how you're growing, and temperature. Most are based on transplant date, so add 2–6 weeks if starting from seed.
60–75°F (15–24°C)	n/a	**SB:** If using a good soil, should not need. Otherwise use nitrogen-rich fertilizer (10-5-5) at half strength every other week **HY:** As needed based on daily PPM meter reading	To extend harvest, cut a few outer leaves at a time, allowing inner leaves to continue to grow. For some varieties, if you harvest the whole plant, cut 1" (2.5cm) above soil and it will regrow—look for "cut and come again" varieties. **VARIETIES:** Green Tatsoi (45 days) Hedou Tiny Bok Choy (40 days) Purple Lady Bok Choy (40 days)
65–85°F (18–29°C)	n/a	**SB:** Low-nitrogen fertilizer (5-10-10) once per month **HY:** As needed based on daily PPM meter reading	Pick beans often or they will stop producing. Bush varieties are best for indoor gardening. Provide vertical structure for pole beans. Look for yellow and purple varieties—they're easier to spot on the plant. **VARIETIES:** Porch Pick (snap) (55 days) Stringless Green Pod (snap) (65 days) Mascotte (filet bean-slimmer) (55 days)
75–85°F (24–29°C)	Hand pollinate. Go from male flower to female flower with swab or small artist paintbrush. Works best with at least two plants	**SB:** Heavy feeder! Balanced fertilizer (10-10-10) at planting, then half strength every other week **HY:** As needed based on daily PPM meter reading	Choose short-season, container or dwarf varieties. Pick cucumbers often or they will stop producing. Choose cucumbers based on intended use—eating/slicing or pickling. Some are good for both. **VARIETIES:** Bush Slicer (60 days) Patio Snacker (60 days)
75–85°F (24–29°C)	Hand pollinate. Go from flower to flower with swab or small artist paintbrush	**SB:** Half strength low-nitrogen fertilizer (5-10-10) every other week **HY:** As needed based on daily PPM meter reading	Choose short-season, container or dwarf varieties. Eggplants come in a multitude of sizes, shapes, and colors (purple, lavender, white, red, orange, green). **VARIETIES:** Patio Mini Baby Eggplant (purple oval) (45 days) Gretel (white elongated) (55 days) Turkish Orange (small round) (85 days) Little Prince (tiny purple) (65 days)
65–85°F (18–29°C)	n/a	**SB:** If using a good soil, should not need additional fertilizer. Otherwise use nitrogen-rich fertilizer (10-5-5) at half strength every other week **HY:** As needed based on daily PPM meter reading	Leaf lettuces grow better than tight head lettuces such as iceberg. To extend harvest, cut a few outer leaves at a time, allowing inner leaves to continue to grow. Grow until leaves start to taste bitter. **VARIETIES:** **Look for these major types:** Bibb, Boston, loose-leaf, butterhead, green leaf, red leaf, Romaine Can be harvested at any stage after a couple inches tall (around 45 days)

VEGETABLES	Info and Growing Method(s)	Light	Water
Peas	**Height:** bush 2'–3' (0.6–1m); climbing 6'–8' (1.8–2.4m) **Plant spacing:** 3" (7.5cm) **Seed depth:** ½"–1" (1.3–2.5cm) (bush needs short support; vining needs trellis) **Seed to transplant:** 28 days (best to plant directly) **Harvest:** 60–80 days from seed **SB:** shallow-rooted; well-drained soil with a lot of compost **Best soil pH:** 6.0–7.5 **HY:** AERO, DS	**FS** in morning **PS** in afternoon 6–8 hrs or **FSGL or BGL:** 8–10 hrs	Moist but not soggy soil when plants are young. Water deeply about once a week when established
Peppers (Hot)	**Height:** 1'–6' (0.3–1.8m) **Plant spacing:** 12"–18" (30–45cm) **Seed depth:** ¼" (0.6cm) (stake or cage at time of planting) **Seed to transplant:** 21–28 days **Harvest:** 90–150 from transplant **SB:** fertile, well-draining soil **Best soil pH:** 6.5–7.0 **HY:** AERO, DS	Needs supplemental light **FS:** 8 hrs + 4–6 hrs supp. or **FSGL or RGL:** 12–16 hrs	Moist but not soggy soil. Dry soil could cause the flowers to drop off
Peppers (Sweet)	**Height:** 1'–6' (0.3–1.8m) **Plant spacing:** 12"–18" (30–45cm) **Seed depth:** ¼" (0.6cm) (stake or cage at time of planting) **Seed to transplant:** 21–28 days **Harvest:** 60–90 from transplant **SB:** fertile, well-draining soil **Best soil pH:** 6.5–7.0 **HY:** AERO, DS	Needs supplemental light **FS:** 8 hrs + 4–6 hrs supp. or **FSGL or RGL:** 12–16 hrs	Moist but not soggy soil. Dry soil could cause the flowers to drop off
Root Vegetables (radishes, carrots, beets, etc.)	**Height:** varies wildly **Plant spacing:** varies wildly from 2"–1' (5cm–0.3m) **Seed depth:** ½" (1.3cm) **Harvest:** varies wildly (root veggies don't like to be transplanted) **SB:** check seed packet for best soil structure and final spacing requirements **Best soil pH:** 6.0–6.5 **HY:** AERO, NFT	Needs supplemental light **FS:** 8–10 hrs or **FSGL or BGL:** 10–12 hrs	Moist but not soggy soil. Water deeply twice a week to encourage roots to reach downward
Tomatoes	**Height:** dwarf 8"–12" (20–30cm); bush 3'–4' (1–1.2m); vining 5'–15' (1.5–4.6m) **Plant spacing:** 18"–24" (45–60cm) (bush/determinate); 12"–18" (30–45cm) (vining/indeterminate varieties that are pruned and suckered) **Seed depth:** ⅛"–¼" (0.3–0.6cm) (stake or trellis at time of planting) **Seed to transplant:** 42–49 days **Harvest:** 50–80+ days from transplant **SB:** fertile, well-draining soil **Best soil pH:** 6.0–7.0 **HY:** AERO, DS, DWC, EFS, NFT	Needs supplemental light **FS:** 8 hrs + 4–6 hrs supp. or **FSGL or RGL:** 12–16 hrs	Moist but not soggy soil. About 1"–2" (2.5–5cm) of water per week

Temperature	Pollination	Fertilizer	Notes
65–75°F (18–24°C)	n/a	**SB:** Should not need, but you may use a balanced fertilize (10-10-10) once when seedlings begin to appear **HY:** As needed based on daily PPM meter reading	Pick peas often or they will stop producing. **VARIETIES:** There are three main types. **Snow:** edible pod, small seeds; Little Marvel, Green Arrow (65 days) **English (a.k.a. Shelling Peas):** round peas you need to take out of the pod (think canned peas); Daybreak (55 days) **Sugar Snap:** larger peas inside an edible pod; Snowbird (40-60 days)
75–85°F (24–29°C)	Hand pollinate. Go from flower to flower with swab or small artist paintbrush	**SB:** Low-nitrogen (5-10-10) fertilizer when transplanting and again when first fruit appears **HY:** As needed based on daily PPM meter reading	Choose short-season, container or dwarf varieties. When plants are about 6" (15cm) tall, snip off the top tip of the plant to encourage bushier growth. **VARIETIES:** Chinese Five-Color Hot Peppers (85 days) Habanero (100–120 days) Numex Lemon Spice (yellow jalapeño) (65 days)
75–85°F (24–29°C)	Hand pollinate. Go from flower to flower with swab or small artist paintbrush	**SB:** Balanced fertilizer (10-10-10) at planting and a low-nitrogen fertilizer when flowers first appear **HY:** As needed based on daily PPM meter reading	Choose short-season, container or dwarf varieties. When plants are about 6" (15cm) tall, snip off the top tip of the plant to encourage bushier growth. **VARIETIES:** Big Dipper (60–90 days) Shishito (60–80 days) Sweet Chocolate Bell (85 days)
65–75°F (18–24°C)	n/a	**SB:** Not needed, but you can use potassium-rich, low-nitrogen fertilizer (0-10-10) once when green tops are about 1" (2.5cm) tall **HY:** As needed based on daily PPM meter reading	Some root vegetable varieties like growing medium that is sandy and other like clay soil—read the seed packet. **VARIETIES:** Too many to name **Carrots:** match variety based on soil (clay, sandy, etc.) (70–80 days) **Radishes:** choose based on preferred "spiciness" (roast for milder flavor) (20–40 days) **Beets:** some are eaten primarily for the bulb and some for the greens (50–60 days)
70–85°F (21–29°C)	Hand pollinate. Go from flower to flower with swab or small artist paintbrush	**SB:** Heavy feeder! Low-nitrogen (0-10-10) or high-phosphorus (5-10-5) fertilizer at time of planting and again when you start to see fruits. After that, half strength every other week **HY:** As needed based on daily PPM meter reading	Choose short-season, container, dwarf, or micro-dwarf varieties. Indeterminate varieties ripen a few at a time—generally vining tomatoes. Determinate tomatoes ripen within a few days and are great for sauces and salsa—usually bush varieties. **VARIETIES:** Yellow Pear (70–80 days) Micro Tom (75 days) Siberia (50 days)

HERBS	Info and Growing Method(s)	Light
	Info varies widely based on variety See online seed seller for best info **SB** = Soil-Based **HY** = Hydroponic	**FS** = Full Sun **PS** = Part Sun **FSGL** = Full-Spectrum Grow Lights **BGL** = Blue Grow Lights **RGL** = Red Grow Lights
Basil	**Height:** dwarf 4"–6" (10–15cm); avg. 6"–24" (15–60cm) **Plant spacing:** 4"–8" (10–20cm) **Seed depth:** ¼" (0.6cm) **Seed to transplant:** 21–28 days **Harvest:** annual; harvest by cutting off leaf tips often; dwarf at 3"–5" (7.5–12.7cm), avg. at 6"–8" (15–20cm) **SB:** shallow-rooted; rich, moist, but well-draining soil **Best soil pH:** 6.0–7.5 **HY:** All hydroponic methods	**FS:** 6–8 hrs or **FSGL or BGL:** 12 hrs
Catnip (bonus plant, not featured in a plant profile)	**Height:** 2'–3' (0.6–1m) **Plant spacing:** 18"–24" (45–60cm). Tip: place seeds in freezer overnight, then soak them in warm water 12–24 hours before planting **Seed depth:** ⅛" (0.3cm) **Seed to transplant:** 14–21 days **Harvest:** perennial; harvest when plant is at least 6" (15cm) tall, but better after plant blooms **SB:** rich, well-draining soil **Best soil pH:** 6.0–7.5 **HY:** All hydroponic methods	**FS:** 4–6 hrs or **FSGL or BGL:** 8–12 hrs
Chives	**Height:** 12" (30cm) **Plant spacing:** 2" (5cm) **Seed depth:** ¼" (0.6cm) **Seed to transplant:** 14–21 days **Harvest:** perennial; harvest when at least 6" (15cm) tall or 30 days after transplanting. Blossoms are also edible. Cut whole plant to 1" (2.5cm) above ground—it will regrow **SB:** shallow-rooted; likes average, well-draining soil **Best soil pH:** 6.0–7.0 **HY:** All hydroponic methods	**FS or PS:** 8–12 hrs or **FSGL or BGL:** 12–16 hrs
Cilantro/ Coriander	**Height:** 18"–24" (45–60cm) **Plant spacing:** 12"–18" (30–45cm) **Seed depth:** ¼"–½" (0.6–1.3cm) **Seed to transplant:** 14–21 days **Harvest:** annual; harvest around 28–42 days; cut leaf tips when 4"–6" (10–15cm) tall; plant every 2–3 weeks (doesn't last long) **SB:** shallow-rooted; fast-draining, light soil with vermiculite, perlite, or sand **Best soil pH:** 6.0–7.0 **HY:** All hydroponic methods	**PS:** 8 hrs Likes afternoon shade, so an east-facing window is good or **FSGL or BGL:** 12 hrs
Dill (bonus plant, not featured in a plant profile)	**Height:** 2'–4' (0.6–1.2m) **Plant spacing:** 12" (30cm) **Seed depth:** ¼" (0.6cm) **Seed to transplant:** 20–28 days **Harvest:** annual; harvest when plant has 4–5 leaves; plant every 2–3 weeks for continuous supply **SB:** shallow-rooted; rich, well-draining soil **Best soil pH:** 5.5–6.5 **HY:** All hydroponic methods	**FS:** 6–8 hrs or **FSGL or BGL:** 8–12 hrs

Water	Temperature	Pollination	Fertilizer	Notes
				Tips. Rather than "varieties," we'll feature basic "types" of herbs. Days to maturity will vary wildly based on variety, how you're growing, and temperature. Most are based on transplant date, so add 2–6 weeks if starting from seed.
Water deeply, about 1" (2.5cm) of water, once a week or more if you see it wilting	65–85°F (18–29°C)	n/a	Not really needed. If desired, use a balanced fertilizer (5-5-5), half-strength, every 6 weeks, not on the leaves	Annual. For all types of basil, harvest the tips of each stem of the plant frequently to produce a bushier plant. Cut flower stalks before blossoms form for longer-lasting harvest. **TYPES:** Italian, Thai, sweet, green, and purple are just some of the types of basil. They all have different flavor profiles (50–60 days)
Water deeply every other week	55–85°F (13–29°C)	n/a	Balanced fertilizer (5-5-5), half-strength, every 6 weeks, not on the leaves	Perennial. Harvest individual leaves as needed after plant is 6" (15cm) tall, or cut the entire plant 2" (5cm) above the soil so it will grow back. Catnip and catmint are not the same. If you want a treat for your cat, you're looking for catnip. **TYPES:** True, Greek, camphor, lemon (85–100 days)
Water regularly. Allow soil to dry out slightly before watering	60–75°F (15–24°C)	n/a	Doesn't need much fertilizer. Balanced fertilizer (5-5-5), half-strength, every 6 weeks, not on the leaves	Perennial. Harvest leaves at any time. Cut close to the soil. Flowers are edible. Divide plants every 3–4 years. **TYPES:** Common, garlic, Siberian (60 days)
Check every couple of days. Water to 1" (2.5cm) deep	60–70°F (15–21°C)	n/a	Balanced fertilizer (5-5-5), half-strength, every 6 weeks, not on the leaves	Annual. Pinch 1" (2.5cm) from tips of plant for fuller growth. Harvest early. It will only last about a month before the flavor changes and flowers appear, so replant every few weeks for a continuous supply. Culantro is a cousin of cilantro. **TYPES:** Leaf, Mexican coriander, Vietnamese (45–70 days)
1"–2" (2.5–5cm) of water per week. Don't allow soil to dry out, but make sure it's not too wet	70–85°F (21–29°C)	n/a	Does not need additional fertilizer. If it starts to look weak, repot with fresh soil	Perennial. Harvest leaves (fronds) frequently. Dill is most potent right before plant flowers. Snip flower stalks or allow to go to seed. **TYPES:** All 50 days **Most common:** bouquet, delikat **Compact types:** fernleaf, compatto **Slow bolt types:** deldukat, elephant, greensleeves, Hera

HERBS	Info and Growing Method(s)	Light
Mint	**Height:** 1'–3' (0.3–1m) **Plant spacing:** 18" (45cm). Mint should never be in the same planter as other crops **Seed depth:** on top of soil to ⅛" (0.3cm) **Seed to transplant:** direct sowing is best **Harvest:** start harvesting when stems are 4" (10cm) tall; most intense flavor just before plant blooms. Perennial; when plant starts to look dead, cut the whole plant to just above second set of leaves and it will regrow in a few weeks **SB:** shallow-rooted; soil should be rich **Best soil pH:** 6.0–7.0 **HY:** All hydroponic methods	**PS:** 6–8 hrs or **FSGL or BGL:** 8–12 hrs
Oregano	**Height:** 1"–2" (2.5–5cm) **Plant spacing:** 12" (30cm) **Seed depth:** ¼" (0.6cm) **Seed to transplant:** 30 days **Harvest:** Perennial. Snip ends of stems when 3" (7.5cm) tall **SB:** shallow-rooted; rich, well-drained soil **Best soil pH:** 6.5–7.0 **HY:** All hydroponic methods	**FS:** 8–12 hrs or **FSGL or BGL:** 12 hrs
Parsley	**Height:** 1'–2' (0.3–0.6m) **Plant spacing:** 2" (5cm) **Seed depth:** ⅛"–¼" (0.3–0.6cm); may benefit from soaking seeds overnight **Seed to transplant:** 40 days (make sure plant has at least three sets of leaves) **Harvest:** when plants are at least 6" (15cm) tall. Tip: biennial, but treat as an annual unless you want to gather seeds **SB:** rich, fast-draining, light soil with vermiculite, perlite, or sand **Best soil pH:** 6.0–7.0 **HY:** All hydroponic methods	**FS or PS:** 6–8 hrs or **FSGL or BGL:** 12–16 hrs
Rosemary	**Height:** 3' (1m) and higher (unless pruned) **Plant spacing:** 2'–3' (0.6–1m) **Seed depth:** ¼" (0.6cm); can take up to 25 days to germinate, so be patient (best to buy transplants or start from cuttings) **Seed to transplant:** 6–8 weeks **Harvest:** perennial; harvest about 6 weeks after transplanting **SB:** shallow-rooted; fast-draining light soil with vermiculite, perlite, or sand. Prefers hot and dry conditions. Indoors it will grow around 14" (35cm) tall and 12" (30cm) wide **Best soil pH:** 6.0–7.0 **HY:** All hydroponic methods	**FS:** 8–12 hrs or **FSGL or BGL:** 12–16
Sage	**Height:** 12"–24" (30–60cm) **Plant spacing:** 24" (60cm) **Seed depth:** on top of soil to ⅛" (0.3cm); needs light to germinate **Seed to transplant:** up to 30 days **Harvest:** perennial; harvest lightly the first year so plant becomes strong, then snip a few leaves as needed **SB:** rich, well-draining soil. Can be 12"–24" (30–60cm) tall and 24" (60cm) wide. Control growth with frequent harvesting **Best soil pH:** 6.0–7.0 **HY:** All hydroponic methods	**FS or PS:** 8–12 hrs or **FSGL or BGL:** 12–16 hrs
Thyme	**Height:** 4"–12" (10–30cm) **Plant spacing:** 12"–24" (30–60cm) **Seed depth:** ¼" (0.6cm) **Seed to transplant:** 28 days **Harvest:** perennial; harvest lightly the first year for a stronger plant; cut the whole plant when flowers are just about to open, leaving 4" (10cm) above ground **SB:** shallow-rooted; fast-draining, light soil with vermiculite, perlite, or sand. Prefers hot and dry conditions. Height and width are around 6"–12" (15–30cm) **Best soil pH:** 6.0–8.0 **HY:** All hydroponic methods	**FS or PS:** 8–12 hrs or **FSGL or BGL:** 12–16 hrs

Water	Temperature	Pollination	Fertilizer	Notes
Keep soil moist, but not soggy. 1"–2" (2.5–5cm) of water per week	55–70°F (13–21°C)	n/a	Does not need additional fertilizer. If it starts to look weak, repot with fresh soil	Perennial. Mint is invasive—grow alone in a container. Harvest the tips of the plant frequently so the plant will be bushy. Cut flower stalk before blossoms form. Some other members of the mint family are pennyroyal, catmint, watermint, and field mint. **TYPES:** Peppermint, spearmint, apple, chocolate, orange, grapefruit, licorice, and many more (90 days)
About 2" (5cm) of water per week. Water when top of soil is dry	55–70°F (13–21°C)	n/a	Balanced fertilizer (5-5-5), half-strength, every month, not on the leaves	Perennial. Clip leaves frequently after plant is 4" (10cm) tall. Don't allow it to flower or the stems will become hard (woody). Some types of oregano have the word "marjoram" in their name, but they are different. If you want marjoram, look for knotted or sweet marjoram. **TYPES:** Common/Greek, Syrian, golden, Italian, Cuban, Mexican (80–90 days)
Water deeply once a week to a depth of 1"–2" (2.5–5cm). Allow to partially dry between waterings	60–70°F (15–21°C)	n/a	Balanced fertilizer (5-5-5), half-strength, every 6 weeks, not on the leaves	Biennial. Harvest the tips of the plant frequently. Cut flower stalks before blossoms form. The two major types of parsley mentioned below have very different textures and flavor profiles. **TYPES:** Curly/curled (70–90 days) Flat-leaf/broad/Italian (70–90 days)
Water lightly, then allow to dry out. It is better to underwater than overwater rosemary. It takes in moisture through its foliage, so generously mist the plant every other day	70–85°F (21–29°C)	n/a	Balanced fertilizer (5-5-5), half-strength, every 6 weeks, not on the leaves	Perennial. Harvest the tips of the plant frequently. Rosemary is called an upside-down plant because the soil can be dry, but its foliage should be frequently misted. **TYPES:** IMPORTANT! Rosemary is a member of the rosmarinus family. Make sure you're getting cullinary rosemary (*Rosmarinus officinalis*) and not ornamental/landscape types. Stick with those called ommon, culinary, or garden rosemary (100–180 days)
Water lightly, then allow to dry out. Drought tolerant	60–70°F (15–21°C)	n/a	Doesn't like too much fertilizer. You can add extra compost around the plant. If you wish to fertilize, use a balanced fertilizer (5-5-5), half-strength, every 6 weeks, not on the leaves	Perennial. Harvest the tips of the plant frequently. Sage does not like to be heavily pruned. Never cut stems to the ground. **TYPES:** IMPORTANT! Sage is a member of the salvia family. Make sure you're getting culinary sage (*Salvia officinalis*) and not ornamental/landscape varieties. Stick with those called common, culinary, or garden sage (75 days)
Water lightly, then allow to dry out	70–85°F (21–29°C)	n/a	Balanced fertilizer (5-5-5), half-strength, every 6 weeks, not on the leaves	Perennial. Harvest 2" (5cm) sections of stems frequently. **TYPES:** Common, lemon, wooly, creeping, wild, elfin (75–90 days)

FRUITS	Info and Growing Method(s)	Light
	Dwarf varieties recommended Transplants recommended **SB** = Soil-Based **HY** = Hydroponics (**AERO** = Aeroponics; **DS** = Drip System; **NFT** = Nutrient Film Technique)	**FS** = Full Sun **PS** = Part Sun **FSGL** = Full-Spectrum Grow Lights **BGL** = Blue Grow Lights **RGL** = Red Grow Lights
Avocados	**Height:** 6'–12' (1.8–3.6m) **Width:** 4'–8' (1.2–2.4m) **Harvest:** 2–7 years (grafted trees will usually produce more quickly) **SB:** when plant arrives, move it to a container twice the width of the roots. Rich but slightly sandy soil **Best soil pH:** 5.0–7.0	**FS:** south-facing window Turn pot weekly 8–12 hrs or **FSGL:** 12–16 hrs
Bananas	**Height:** 5'–10' (1.5–3m) **Width:** 4'–8' (1.2–2.4m) **Harvest:** 1–2 years **SB:** when plant arrives, move it to a container twice the width of the roots. Keep up-potting until you reach a 15-gallon (56L) pot. It does not like to start out in a large pot. Use a slightly acidic soil **Best soil pH:** 5.5–6.5	**FS or PS:** south- or west-facing window (afternoon sun) Turn pot weekly 12 hrs or **FSGL:** 12–18 hrs
Blueberries	**Height:** dwarf 1'–3' (0.3–1m) **Width:** 2'–4' (0.6–1.2m) **Harvest:** 2–3 years **SB:** in a pot at least 18" (45cm) deep and wide. Blueberries like an acidic soil, so buy a special soil **Best soil pH:** 4.5–5.5 **HY:** NFT	**FS:** 6–8 hrs or **FSGL:** 12–16 hrs
Cherries	**Height:** 8'–10' (2.4–3m) **Width:** 6'–10' (1.8–3m) **Harvest:** about 3 years **SB:** lighter, sandy soil, in a 15-gallon (56L) pot **Best soil pH:** 6.5–7.0 **HY:** AERO, DS	**FS or PS:** 6 hrs or **FSGL:** 12–16 hrs
Figs	**Height:** 30"–12' (0.8–3.6m) **Width:** 30"–12' (0.8–3.6m) **Harvest:** 3–5 years **SB:** start with a pot only one size larger than the original container and keep up-potting as needed. Soil should have a lot of rich organic material **Best soil pH:** 5.5–6.5"	**FS:** 6–8 hrs or **FSGL:** 12–16 hrs

Water	Temperature/Chill Hours	Pollination	Fertilizer	Notes
				Tips and a few suggested varieties. Days to maturity will vary wildly based on variety or general type, how you're growing, what size tree you purchase, and temperature.
Keep moist early on. After established, allow soil to dry between watering. Water weekly thoroughly. Mist leaves daily	60–85°F (15–29°C) No chill hrs	Self-fertile, but will grow better with two plants and hand pollination. Go from flower to flower with swab or small artist paintbrush	Do not fertilize during first year. Then, well-balanced (5-5-5) fertilizer twice a year	Dwarf varieties are suggested. Prune dead branches. Stake when planting and tie loosely as it grows. **VARIETIES:** **Wurtz a.k.a. Little Cado:** H=6'–12' (1.8–3.6m); W=4'–8' (1.2–2.4m) **Condo:** H=8'–10' (2.4–3m); W=5' (1.5m)
Water twice a week or when soil is dry 2"–3" (5–7.5cm) down. Water close to the soil, as the leaves can redirect the water away from the roots	75–85°F (24–29°C) No chill hrs	Self-fertile, but will grow better with two plants and hand pollination. Go from flower to flower with swab or small artist paintbrush	Compost or a balanced or high-potassium fertilizer (5-5-5 or 5-5-10) once a month	Dwarf varieties are suggested. When bananas start to sprout, cut off main flower to encourage larger growth. **VARIETIES:** **Dwarf Cavendish Banana:** H=8'–10' (2.4–3m); W=4'–5' (1.2–1.5m)
Moist but not soggy soil. Soil needs to be moist 2"–3" (5–7.5cm) down. Check moisture every few days. You'll probably need to water once a week	45–80°F (7–27°C) 550 chill hrs	Self-fertile, but will grow better with two plants and hand pollination. Go from flower to flower with swab or small artist paintbrush	Does not need fertilizer the first year. Thereafter, use a 4-3-6 fertilizer specifically for acid-loving plants	Dwarf/compact, self-fertile varieties are suggested. If lower limbs touch the soil, prune them off. Also remove dead branches. **VARIETIES:** **Top Hat Blueberry Bush:** H=1'–2' (0.3–0.6m); W=1'–2' (0.3–0.6m) **Northblue Dwarf:** H=2'–3' (0.6–1m); W=2'–3' (0.6–1m)
Moist but not soggy soil. Allow soil to dry slightly between watering	45–80°F (7–27°C) 700 chill hrs	Self-fertile, but will grow better with two plants and hand pollination. Go from flower to flower with swab or small artist paintbrush	Fertilize lightly with a low-nitrogen fertilizer (5-10-10) only after tree starts fruiting, then only once a year	Dwarf varieties are suggested. **VARIETIES:** **Carmine Jewel:** H=6'–8' (1.8–2.4m); W=6'–8' (1.8–2.4m) **Juliette Dwarf:** H=5'–8' (1.5–2.4m); W=5'–8' (1.5–2.4m)
Moist but not soggy soil. Allow soil to dry between watering	50–85°F (10–29°C) 100 chill hrs	Self-fertile, but will grow better with two plants and hand pollination. Go from flower to flower with swab or small artist paintbrush	Fertilize twice a year with a balanced fertilizer (8-8-8). A slow-release fertilizer is a good option	Dwarf varieties are suggested. **VARIETIES:** **Fignomental Fig:** H=2½' (0.8m) **Celestial:** H=10' (3m) (can be pruned)

FRUITS	Info and Growing Method(s)	Light
Lemons	**Height:** 3'–6' (1–1.8m) **Width:** 3'–4' (1–1.2m) **Harvest:** 2–3 years **SB:** start with a pot only one size larger than the original container and keep up-potting as needed. Thrives in loamy or sandy soil **Best soil pH:** 5.5–6.5	**FS:** 8 hrs or **FSGL:** 16 hrs
Oranges	**Height:** 4'–8' (1.2–2.4m) **Width:** 2'–3' (0.6–1m) **Harvest:** 2–3 years **SB:** start with a pot only one size larger than the original container and keep up-potting as needed. Will grow in a variety of soils **Best soil pH:** 6.0–7.5	**FS:** 8–10 hrs or **FSGL:** 12–16 hrs
Peaches	**Height:** 6' (1.8m) **Width:** 6' (1.8m) **Harvest:** 2–4 years **SB:** start with a pot only one size larger than the original container and keep up-potting as needed **Best soil pH:** 6.5–7.0 **HY:** AERO, DS	**FS:** 6–8 hrs or **FSGL:** 12–16 hrs
Pomegranates	**Height:** 2'–4' (0.6–1.2m) **Width:** 2'–3' (0.6–1m) **Harvest:** 3–4 years **SB:** rich but slightly sandy soil. A 10-gallon (38L) pot should do **Best soil pH:** 5.5–7.0	**FS:** 6 hrs or **FSGL:** 12 hrs
Raspberries	**Height:** 2'–4' (0.6–1.2m) **Width:** 2'–4' (0.6–1.2m) **Harvest:** 2 years **SB:** rich but slightly sandy soil. Dwarf varieties need a minimum of a 5-gallon (19L) pot **Best soil pH:** 5.5–6.5	**FS:** 6–8 hrs or **FSGL:** 12–16 hrs
Strawberries (also featured in a plant profile)	**Height:** 6"–8" (15–20cm) **Width:** 12"–18" (30–45cm) **Harvest:** first year **SB:** rich but slightly sandy soil. Shallow rooted. Individual plants can be put in a 6" (15cm) pot. Plant about 8" (20cm) apart in larger containers **Best soil pH:** 5.5–6.5 **HY:** AERO, DS, NFT	**FS:** 6–8 hrs or **FSGL:** 12–16 hrs

Water	Temperature/Chill Hours	Pollination	Fertilizer	Notes
Moist but not soggy soil. Check 2"–3" (5–7.5cm) down into the soil and water when it's dry	50–85°F (10–29°C) No chill hrs	Self-fertile, but will grow better with two plants and hand pollination. Go from flower to flower with swab or small artist paintbrush	Fertilize twice a year with a fertilizer specifically for citrus	Dwarf varieties are suggested. **VARIETIES:** **Meyer Lemon:** H=4'–6' (1.2–1.8m)
Moist but not soggy soil. Check 2"–3" (5–7.5cm) down into the soil and water when it's dry	50–85°F (10–29°C) No chill hrs	Self-fertile, but will grow better with two plants and hand pollination. Go from flower to flower with swab or small artist paintbrush	Fertilize twice a year with a fertilizer specifically for citrus	Dwarf varieties are suggested. **VARIETIES:** **Dwarf Calamondin:** H=6'–10' (1.8–3m) (can be pruned)
Moist but not soggy soil. Check 2"–3" (5–7.5cm) down into the soil and water when it's dry	50–85°F (10–29°C) 450–1,200 chill hrs (depending on variety)	Self-fertile, but will grow better with two plants and hand pollination. Go from flower to flower with swab or small artist paintbrush	Use a high-nitrogen fertilizer (10-5-5) the first two years, then a balanced fertilizer (10-10-10) can be used. Fertilize when blossoms form, again two months later, then again after harvesting	Dwarf varieties are suggested. **VARIETIES:** **Belle of Georgia:** H=8'–10' (2.4–3m)
Moist but not soggy soil. At least 1" (2.5cm) of water is needed per week	50–90°F (10–32°C) 150–200 chill hrs	Self-fertile, but will grow better with two plants and hand pollination. Go from flower to flower with swab or small artist paintbrush	Use a high-nitrogen fertilizer (10-5-5) when planting, then fertilize annually when you see signs of new growth	Dwarf varieties are suggested. **VARIETIES:** **Dwarf Red:** H=8'–10' (2.4–3m); W=8'–10' (2.4–3m) (can be pruned)
Moist but not soggy soil. At least 2" (5cm) of water is needed per week. More when fruiting	65–75°F (18–24°C) 800 chill hrs	Self-fertile, but will grow better with two plants and hand pollination. Go from flower to flower with swab or small artist paintbrush	Use a high-nitrogen fertilizer (10-5-5) when planting, then fertilize annually when you see signs of new growth	Dwarf varieties are suggested. **VARIETIES:** **Raspberry Shortcake:** H=2'–3' (0.6–1m); W=3'–4' (1–1.2m) **Heritage Everbearing:** H=5'–6' (1.5–1.8m); W=3'–4' (1–1.2m)
Moist but not soggy soil for the first few weeks. Once established, deep but infrequent watering. Allow soil to dry between waterings	50–80°F (10–27°C) No chill hrs	Self-fertile, but will grow better with two plants and hand pollination. Go from flower to flower with swab or small artist paintbrush	Balanced fertilizer (5-5-5), half-strength, every two weeks, not on the leaves. High-nitrogen fertilizer (10-5-5) after harvest	There are three main types of strawberries. **TYPES:** **June-bearing:** all fruits ripen within a few days of each other. These varieties are best if you need them all ready at once to make a pie or jam. (20–30 days from bare root) **Everbearing:** fruits ripen a few at a time over a longer period of time. (30–40 days from bare root) **Day-neutral** (25–35 days from bare root)

Vegetables, Roots, and Leaves

Asian Greens

There is no easy way to describe Asian greens—just know that these easy-to-grow plants encompass many leafy members of the Brassica family, which we normally think of as the broccoli/cabbage family. Some of the familiar names are bok choy, mizuna, mustard greens, and tatsoi, but those just scratch the surface. Colors range from pale greens all the way to a very dark purple that almost looks black, and sizes range from mini to over 2' (60cm) across. Leaves can be thin and tender with jagged edges to a sturdy paddle shape, and flavors range from mild to sinus-clearing spicy. Try growing any kind you like, plant at least two plants at a time, and start new plants every 2–3 weeks—whichever species you choose, they are all nutrition powerhouses. Just like lettuces, you can cut a couple outer leaves from each plant and allow the center to continue to grow for a longer harvest.

Asian greens appreciate regular watering—the soil should be moist but not too wet. Depending on the variety and how early you want to harvest them, they will be ready in 20–50 days.

Growing Guidelines	Full sun/light to part shade. Direct sow or seed 4–5 weeks ahead of time in trays to transplant. Sow seeds ¼" (0.6cm) deep, with a bright light source. Keep moist.
Fertilizer	High nitrogen, half strength, every other week
Pests	Aphids, thrips, caterpillars
Diseases	Generally disease-free

Bok choy

Beans (Fresh)

For growing indoors, I prefer bush beans because they don't grow as tall. Like tomatoes, beans come in indeterminate and determinate varieties. Bush beans are determinate, which means that they'll all be ready to harvest at about the same time. If you are a bean lover, start a new plant every week or two so you have a continuous supply. If space is a premium, look for a container variety.

If you do choose a vining or pole bean, you'll need to provide a trellis for it to grow up. Since they are indeterminate, they will only produce a few beans at a time, so two to four plants will be needed to have a full serving. As soon as they are ready to harvest, pick them. Don't wait for more to become ready—if you don't pick them frequently, it's a signal to the plant to stop producing. Start new plants every 3–4 weeks. Beans are notorious for hiding on the plant, so I often choose yellow or purple varieties so I can spot them easier. Purple beans are gorgeous, but they turn green when you cook them.

Since beans are shallow-rooted veggies, you can plant them in a shallow container. When picking them, be sure to hold the plant firmly, or you may end up pulling the plant out of the soil. They're most flavorful eaten raw, but they are also good steamed.

Growing Guidelines	Full sun/light. Direct sow only, 1" (2.5cm) deep. Water deeply but less frequently.
Fertilizer	Light feeders, half-strength fertilizer every other month
Pests	Aphids
Diseases	Blight, mildew, rust

Beets

Make sure the variety you plan to grow is small enough for your container, as some beets can get quite large, and some even grow long like carrots. Most beets are deep red in color, but golden beets are also wonderful. With most varieties, the seeds are actually in clusters, so you can get away with only plantings one cluster per planting hole—be prepared to thin by cutting out unwanted plants instead of pulling. If you have space, you can grow several beets at the same time, as you can keep them in the ground for a while and pull them when you're ready for them. Don't forget to eat the greens.

While some people are successful at transplanting beets, I've found that the beets do better if you direct sow them in their permanent home. You can cut down on the time by soaking the seed clusters in water overnight. Don't be surprised to see the top of the beet peeking up above the ground—that's its normal growing habit.

Beets are quick growing and are ready from seed to harvest in 50–60 days in most cases. I like to harvest them earlier while they are smaller or grow a smaller variety when I want to can whole pickled beets. They can be cut into quarters and either steamed or, my favorite, roasted in the oven.

If you planted them too closely, thin them out and eat the thinnings. The average beets are between 1"–3" (2.5–7.6cm) in diameter, and the leaves can grow up to 18" (46cm) tall.

See more detail on choosing a variety in Chapter 10.

Growing Guidelines	Full sun/light to part shade. Direct sow only, ½" (1.3cm) deep. Keep moist.
Fertilizer	About two weeks after seeds break through the ground and six weeks later
Pests	Aphids, spider mites
Diseases	Leaf spot, mildew, wilt, rust

Cabbage (Napa)

Napa cabbage (biennial)

Just like lettuce, I don't grow tight round head cabbage, but instead stick with dwarf varieties of Napa cabbage (a.k.a. Chinese cabbage) because of its looser growing habit. It has a milder, sweeter flavor than traditional round cabbages, and the heads (yes, Napa cabbage is also called a head of cabbage) can be harvested before they reach full maturity. Dwarf varieties will grow even more quickly. If I do grow tight head cabbages, I also like smaller dwarf varieties.

Napa cabbage is one of those crops that needs a strong light source to germinate, and they also like even moisture, so one of the small DIY wicking planters shown in Chapter 13 would be ideal to start cabbage seeds. This is another vegetable that likes cooler weather, so I grow it in the winter months and make sure they're close to the window.

Some regular-sized Napa cabbages are up to 10"–20" (25–51cm) tall, while dwarf varieties are usually 8" (20cm) or less in height. They'll be ready about 70–90 days after the seeds sprout.

Napa cabbage is great for stir-fry dishes and making kimchi. I love using the leaves to make sandwich wraps.

Growing Guidelines	Full sun/light. Plant seeds ¼" (0.6cm) deep. You can start seeds in a seeding tray under a strong light, then transplant, or you can direct sow.
Fertilizer	Napa cabbage doesn't require a lot of fertilizer and would be happy with some added compost. Once the head begins to form, you can apply fish emulsion.
Pests	Aphids
Diseases	Leaf spot, rot, various fungal diseases

Carrots

In Chapter 10, we talked about the difference between eating and juicing carrots, so review that information and select the right variety for your intended use.

These yummy root vegetables come in numerous varieties, from small, round ball varieties all the way up to over 2' (61cm) long. They also come in a surprising array of colors, not just orange. The depth of your container determines how long your carrots can be, but I suggest growing varieties that are 8" (20cm) or smaller.

Different varieties of carrots require different types of soil, so consult the directions on the seed packet for the best advice. They are best sown directly rather than from transplant. Depending on the variety, they should be ready to harvest anywhere from 50–75 days. Don't be surprised to see the tops of the carrots above the soil line—that's completely natural.

Unlike many vegetables, harvesting carrots young is not a good idea, as the roots will be bland. Those cute baby carrots you see in the grocery store are either a special variety or they are larger carrots that have been whittled down to a uniform size and shape.

Although rare, some people are highly sensitive to carrot foliage and show signs of skin irritation if they come into contact with it. If you really love carrots but have that sensitivity, wear gloves when working with them. If you're not sensitive, carrots tops are also edible.

Growing Guidelines	Full sun/light to part shade. Barely cover seeds with no more than ¼" (0.6cm) of soil 2"–4" (5–10cm) apart depending on variety. Water consistently.
Fertilizer	If you started out with good soil, you shouldn't need fertilizer. If you want to fertilize, choose one with low nitrogen.
Pests	Carrot rust flies
Diseases	Leaf spot, leaf blight, bacterial soft rot

Cucumbers

Because we're growing in limited spaces, I prefer to grow dwarf bush (container) varieties of cucumbers when indoor gardening. If you want to grow vining cucumbers, be sure to plan for some sort of trellis for the plant to run up. There are a wide variety of vining cucumbers: round and elongated varieties from short and stubby to long and extremely long. The leaves generally have a rough and unpleasant feel to them, and the fruits of many varieties have a spiny texture—these spines usually wipe off easily with a cloth.

No matter what type you grow, if you don't continually pick the ripe cucumbers, they'll stop producing, so enjoy them young. Male blossoms appear first. As soon as the females appear, you'll want to hand pollinate using a small artist's paintbrush or a cotton swab.

Cucumbers like consistent watering. If you don't water them regularly, the fruits may become bitter tasting.

They are called heavy feeders because they need to be started in good, fertile soil, then either have compost added or be fertilized every 3–4 weeks with a low-nitrogen fertilizer—otherwise, you'll produce lovely leaves with fewer fruits.

Unless they're a yellow variety, harvest them before you they start to turn yellow. Don't try to pull them off the vine, but rather cut them so you don't damage the plant.

If you're growing your plants vertically, you can put two in 1 square foot (0.03 square meters) of space. Bush or container cucumbers have different spacing requirements, so consult the seed packet.

The two main types of cucumbers are slicing and pickling. See more detail on choosing a variety in Chapter 10.

Growing Guidelines	Full sun/light. Direct sow or start seeds in trays by planting 1" (2.5cm) deep.
Fertilizer	Every two weeks with a low-nitrogen fertilizer
Pests	Aphids. If you purchase transplants from the store, be sure to check under the leaves for insect eggs—these could be caterpillars.
Diseases	Various mildew and fungal diseases, bacterial wilt, cucumber mosaic

Eggplant

Most of us are used to seeing the large, deep purple pear-shaped or lighter purple narrow varieties, but there is a whole world of sizes, shapes, and colors when it comes to eggplants. Some of my favorites are smaller varieties that come in white, pale green, orange, red, lavender, or dark purple.

If you decide to start seeds in trays, when you move them to their permanent home, place a tall support stake (i.e., a bamboo pole) at time of transplanting, or seeding if you direct sow. As the plant grows, loosely tie it to the stake every few inches (about every 7cm). If you wait to stake them later, you could do irreparable damage to the roots.

Before cooking larger varieties, cut them and sprinkle generously with kosher salt and let them "weep" for 10 minutes before wiping them dry. If you don't, they'll soak up too much oil during baking. You can skip this step with the small varieties.

Eggplants are sun lovers—the more sun, the better. Sun and supplemental lighting should total about 12 hours a day.

In general, the fruit is ready to pick when the skin is glossy and it has a little give when you press on it. Cut them from the step—don't pull. Unlike many other veggies, don't harvest them unless they're ripe.

Growing Guidelines	Full sun/light. Barely cover seeds with ¼" (0.6cm) of soil. Keep the soil moist by gently misting it and cover with plastic food wrap. There's some advantage to starting seeds in cell packs or seed trays on top of a heat mat. They can take up to 2 weeks to germinate, so be patient. Water regularly and consistently.
Fertilizer	Feed diluted liquid fertilizer every other week during the growing season
Pests	Flea beetles
Diseases	Verticillium wilt is not as much of a problem if you use a good, clean soil

Green Onions, Scallions, and Shallots

Each of these are different plants, but all are basically grown the same way. Some are smaller, but the largest can be up to 3' (91cm) tall and 2' (61cm) wide, so check the instructions on the seed packet for planting depth and spacing requirements.

You can plant these every couple of weeks to have a fresh harvest. I like harvesting green onions when they're quite small and pungent. Harvest before the flower stalk appears.

Growing Guidelines	Full sun/light to part shade. Plant seeds about ¼" (0.6cm) deep. Perennial or annual. If you want to grow scallions as a perennial, it's recommended that you don't harvest the first year to allow the plant to become established. It will produce even better the next year. Thin to 2" (5cm) apart. Make sure they're consistently moist but not soggy.
Fertilizer	High nitrogen when planting; can also fertilize half strength monthly
Pests	Onion maggots, thrips, aphids
Diseases	Generally disease-free, but can rarely have leaf blight, powdery mildew, onion smut

Leafy Greens

Don't confuse these with so-called "greens" like beet greens or turnip greens that are cut from the tops of root vegetables. Rather, think of Swiss chard, kale, collards, spinach, arugula, watercress, etc. Some can grow quite large, so look for container varieties.

All of these are easy to grow from seed. Check the seed packet to see how far apart to space the seeds—look for the final spacing directions. The good thing is, if you plant them too closely, you can always harvest one of them early as a baby green. Young greens are marvelous additions to a salad, and mature greens are great stir-fried and soups or braised. Harvest a few outer leaves from each plant for a longer harvest period.

Growing Guidelines	Check packets, as different species have different light needs and planting depths. In general, most varieties like full sun/light but may appreciate afternoon shade if the room is warm. Water well.
Fertilizer	High-nitrogen, every two weeks
Pests	Aphids, thrips, flea beetle/caterpillars
Diseases	Downy mildew, some leaf spot, rot

New Zealand Spinach

Shallots

Lettuce (Leaf)

The common term is to grow a "head" of lettuce, but that can be a little confusing. Lettuces are divided into three main categories: head, loose leaf, and cos. Head lettuce includes any tightly formed variety like iceberg and crisphead. Loose leaf (a.k.a. leaf) is any rounded variety that does not form a tight head. Cos lettuce varieties grow taller and usually have a strong center rib on each leaf, like romaine. I personally don't grow head lettuces because they are more difficult, take more time to grow, don't generally have as many nutrients, and you must harvest the whole plant.

Continuously plant a couple of lettuces per person every other week if you enjoy a daily salad. The best thing about loose leaf and cos lettuce varieties is that you don't have to harvest the full plant. Using a sharp knife, cut a few outer leaves from each plant and let the interior continue to grow for a few more weeks. Eventually, the plant will send up flower stalks and the leaves will start to taste bitter. When this happens, it's time to remove the whole plant.

Growing Guidelines	Partial shade. Direct sow or start seeds in trays, planting seeds ¼" (0.6cm) to ½" (1.3cm) deep, depending on variety. Keep moist.
Fertilizer	When plants first emerge or when transplanting
Pests	Aphids, thrips, caterpillars
Diseases	Fungal diseases

Peas (Dwarf Snap)

I don't think I've ever cooked home-grown peas, because my grandchildren and I always eat them before they can make it to the kitchen. My favorites are English (shelling) peas, which are vining and require trellising. They are the ones you remove the seeds from the pod to cook or enjoy raw. You can grow vining varieties just a couple inches (about 5cm) apart.

The other types of peas are snow peas. These are the ones that are quite flat and used in stir-fries. Sugar snap peas are a hybrid between snow and English. The seeds are small like snow peas, but the pod is fleshy like English peas. They can be eaten raw or cooked whole.

I suggest growing container and dwarf snow and sugar snap peas. These varieties will be less than 30" (76cm) tall and grow well in a 15" (38cm) container spaced about 3" (7.6cm) apart. Use something like a small tomato cage to corral them.

For all varieties, if you don't pick them, the plant will stop producing, so harvest frequently. Start new plants every 3–4 weeks.

Though they can do well in part shade, the more light they get, the better—12 hours of a combination of natural sun and supplemental lighting is ideal.

Growing Guidelines	Full sun/light to part shade. Direct sow only, 1" (2.5cm) deep. Add a small trellis to the container when you plant the peas. Water deeply at least once a week.
Fertilizer	None required
Pests	Not a lot of pest problems, but may be bothered by aphids, thrips, spider mites
Diseases	Fairly disease-free; fusarium wilt and root rot are infrequent

Peppers (Dwarf Hot and Sweet)

Even in the garden, peppers can be a little challenging to grow. They seem to take forever to germinate, with sweet peppers being a little faster than hot. Using a seed tray or small seed cells on a heat mat will speed up germination—check that the soil is moist for good germination.

Peppers like a lot of bright light, so for them to produce fruit, you will need supplemental lighting that includes the red spectrum. They'll need about 12–16 hours of supplemental light every day. I use a timer to ensure they get the proper amount of darkness.

In most cases when you transplant a seedling, you are told to make sure to put the plant into the new pot at the same soil level as before, but with peppers, you'll want to drop them 1" (2.5cm) lower than the original soil level. Roots will form at the base of the plant, which will make it stronger.

Whether direct seeding or transplanting, add a bamboo pole or other stake to the pot at the same time to support the plant by loosely tying the plant to the stake every few inches (about every 7cm). If you wait to stake them later, you could do irreparable damage to the roots.

All colors of peppers start out green and ripen to their final colors. Red, yellow, orange, and purple sweet peppers generally have a different flavor than if you pick them green. Most peppers will be ready about 65–75 days from the time you transplant them.

Whether hot or sweet, dwarf pepper plants are my favorite. The height can range from about 8" (25cm) to 3' (91cm). When they reach final maturity, cut the fruits from the vine instead of trying to pull them off. You might end up with the whole plant in your hand—at the very least, you could damage the plant.

Growing Guidelines	Full sun/light (supplemental lighting will be required). Direct sow or start seeds ¼" (0.6cm) deep.
Fertilizer	Not high in nitrogen, half-strength, every two weeks
Pests	Aphids, thrips
Diseases	Fungal diseases like damping off, blossom end rot, Verticillium rot

Radishes

Radishes come in a variety of shapes (globe, cylindrical, and Asian radishes are carrot-shaped) and colors (bi-color, red, white, pink, purple, and black), with flavors ranging from mild to very spicy. These fast-growing gems are fun and easy for children.

Some Asian radishes, like daikon, can be quite large, so pay attention to the variety you're growing to determine how deep your containers need to be. Radish greens can be cooked and eaten.

Radishes take anywhere from 25–60 days to grow and should be direct sown. Check the seed packet for the final spacing directions; this is how far apart you'll plant them, putting two seeds in each planting hole. If both of the seeds sprout, cut one with a pair of scissors.

If you don't like spicy radishes, look specifically for those labeled as "mild." Another trick is to roast them—they take on a completely different flavor profile than raw radishes.

Growing Guidelines	Full sun/light to part shade. Direct sow only, ½" (1.3cm) deep. Needs consistent water.
Fertilizer	High-nitrogen, at time of planting
Pests	Aphids
Diseases	Several fungal diseases, downy mildew

Strawberries

Strawberries are quite easy to grow indoors. Overcrowding can lead to mold problems, though, so be careful. June-bearing fruits are ready to harvest within a few days of each other, and this is the best option if you want to make a strawberry pie or jam. You'll need several plants that were planted at the same time, but it's doable.

If you want just a couple berries every day for your cereal instead, then ever-bearing varieties are what you want. They generally have two main harvests a year, but they may have additional smaller harvests.

Starting strawberries from seed is quite difficult. To increase your chance of success, you'll need to stratify them in the refrigerator or freezer (read about stratification in Chapter 12). Even then, chances of success can be low. It's much easier to start strawberries from bare root plants. Just remember that plants won't be available year-round.

When you receive the bare-root plants, gently separate them and soak them in a container of water or your kitchen sink for about 30–60 minutes. Prepare a pot that has good drainage by filling it about half full with a damp potting mix that is super light, such as a bagged product with a coco coir base.

Once you have identified the root mass, you'll be able to find the "crown" from which the strawberry plant will grow. The crown must never be buried in the soil, or the plant will rot. You will see a definite line where the roots meet the crown. Hold the crown in one hand while putting the roots in the pot and start pressing more damp soil into the roots. Add more soil until the roots are covered. Holding the crown will ensure that you don't bury it. Water well.

I know this will be hard to do, but it's a good practice to remove all the blossoms from the plants the first year. This will give the plants a chance to establish and increase your harvest significantly in succeeding years.

Regular watering is crucial, especially the period from the time the flowers show until you finish harvesting. Wait for the berries to fully ripen. Once they're fully red, wait another day or two. The good thing is you're not competing with birds and critters like when you plant them outside!

Strawberry plants send out long shoots that are called runners. For June-bearing varieties, leave the runners in place, but cut off the runners on ever-bearing plants.

Growing Guidelines	Full sun/light plus supplemental lighting for a total of 12–16 hours. Less light will result in fewer berries. See above for growing directions.
Fertilizer	Once a month with a potassium-rich fertilizer until the plants flower, then fertilize every ten days until harvesting is complete
Pests	Mites and aphids
Diseases	Fungal diseases can be prevented by good air circulation

Tomatoes

Dwarf Orange Hat Tomato

Both vining and bush tomatoes can be grown in a pot—vining tomatoes will need a tall trellis structure, and bush varieties will need to be staked or caged. Believe it or not, most tomatoes can comfortably be grown in a container just 12" (31cm) across, but wider will be better.

There are several species of container, dwarf, and even micro-dwarf tomatoes nowadays. Incredibly, some of these small plants bear full-sized fruits. Supplemental lighting that includes the red spectrum is required. Depending on the height of your chosen varieties, you'll need some sort of vertical plant support that should be installed at the time of planting so you don't damage the roots. Check out the Dwarf Tomatoes Project (*www.dwarftomatoproject.net*).

See more detail on choosing what tomato to grow for what purpose in Chapter 10, and see how and why to bury them deep in Chapter 12. Then go to Chapter 13 to see about pinching and pruning your tomato plants—it's an optional technique that you can use to control the foliage growth of your plants.

No matter what type of tomato you choose or how you grow it, all tomatoes like consistent watering, so invest in a self-watering or wicking container, or see Chapter 13 for a DIY option. Tomatoes would do great in a 5-gallon (19L) bucket with proper drainage.

Growing Guidelines	See package directions, as each variety is different. Full sun/light. Direct sow or start seeds in a seed tray. Keep evenly moist. Supplemental (red) light is required for 12–16 hours per day.
Fertilizer	Tomatoes are called heavy feeders because they like to be fed every two weeks with a half-strength, low-nitrogen fertilizer. If your fertilizer is high in nitrogen, you'll get very lush leaves with few fruits.
Pests	Aphids, cutworm (not if using new/good soil), leaf hoppers, spider mites, trips, whiteflies
Diseases	Several blights and leaf spot, Verticillium wilt, blossom end rot

NOTE: There are too many possible pest and disease problems to name, and some of them are variety specific. Check the seed packet for your variety, and search online for "tomato diseases with pictures" and "tomato pests with images" to see what might be bothering your plant.

Herbs and Spices

GUIDELINES FOR ALL HERBS AND SPICES

Remove the flowers, or even better the buds, as soon as they appear, unless you intend to collect seeds. Budding signals the plant to stop growing and start producing seeds.

If you've grown too much, put the excess in the blender and puree it. If they are soft-stemmed herbs, add those too, but not the woody stems. Put a dollop of puree into each well of an ice cube tray, then add either water or olive oil and put it in the freezer. Once frozen, they can be transferred to a plastic freezer bag or container—one bag for each herb (don't forget to label them). Water cubes can be thrown into sauces, soups, and stews, while oil cubes are great for sautéing.

Leaves can also be frozen on a cookie sheet. Inspect each leaf and throw away any that show signs of disease. Remove the leaves from the stems, wash, dry, and spread them out in a single layer, giving leaves room so they're not touching (this will be impossible with tiny leaves—just do your best). When frozen, transfer them to a freezer bag.

Herbs can also be dehydrated. Follow the manufacturer's directions for temperature and length of time. You can also look online to see methods for how to dehydrate herbs using your oven.

Fresh and dried leaves can make wonderful herbal teas. Don't just limit yourself to mint—experiment!

Basil

Basil is what's called a short-lived perennial because it rarely lasts more than a couple years, but you may want to think of it as an annual and sow seeds every few weeks for a continual supply.

While most people normally think of sweet basil, there are varieties with a hint of lemon, licorice, and cinnamon, as well as Thai basil, which has a completely different flavor. There are dwarf basils that top out around 8" (20cm) tall and others that reach up to 6' (1.8m) in height, but the average is about 24" (61cm). Leaf size can also vary wildly.

To get a bushier plant, pinch or snip the terminal bud and the top few leaves (see photo). Don't let the flower buds mature. You don't have to wait for buds to form—if your basil plant is leggy, just remove the top part of each stem where you see two other stems branching out. New leaves and branches will quickly form. You can start this pinching process when the plant is about 6" (15cm) tall.

Basil is a plant that likes to be watered deeply and regularly but not have its feet wet, so make sure the soil is very well-draining. It also likes to have its foliage sprayed a couple times a week.

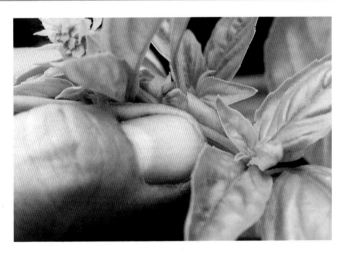

Growing Guidelines	Full sun/light (supplemental lighting will be needed in darker months).
Fertilizer	Use a balanced all-purpose fertilizer monthly or half-strength every two weeks.
Pests	Aphids
Diseases	Powdery mildew

Chives

This perennial herb has an onion-like flavor and is a member of the Allium genus. Garlic chives are similar and have a mild garlic flavor. They're commonly used for salads and to flavor soups, but you can also enjoy their edible flowers. Plants can grow to around 15" (38cm) tall, but they'll be more flavorful if you cut them sooner. When you want to use some chives, grab a small handful and cut them close to the soil. Younger leaves are more tender, so harvest frequently.

These easy-to-grow, shallow-rooted beauties self-seed if you allow the flowers to remain on the plant. It's a good practice to remove the flowers before they begin to seed. The lilac, red, pink, or white flowers are beautiful, so enjoy a bouquet.

Chives can quickly become pot-bound, and you will have to divide the clumps every couple of years. Just remove them from the pot and pull them apart. They're tough plants, so don't worry about harming them. Put one clump back in the pot and either find another pot for the other clump or use/freeze the rest.

At least once a year, give the entire plant a good haircut, all the way to soil level.

Growing Guidelines	Full sun/light. Sow seeds close to the surface—no more than ¼" (0.6cm) deep. Keep evenly moist.
Fertilizer	Not really needed
Pests	Thrips, onion maggots (not a problem if your soil is new/sterilized)
Diseases	Root rot

Cilantro/Coriander

What's the difference between cilantro and coriander? Cilantro refers to the green parts of the plant (stems and leaves), while coriander is the dried seeds of the plant. Both are delicious, unless you're one of the unlucky people who lost the genetic lottery and to whom cilantro tastes like soap.

Unlike most herbs, cilantro likes gentler morning sunlight and then partial shade in the afternoon, as its delicate leaves can get scorched with too much sun. They will certainly not need supplemental lighting.

Plant seeds no more than ¼" (0.6cm) deep and about 6"–12" (15–31cm) apart. Cilantro likes to grow with a friend, so plant at least two plants per pot.

It's a quick-growing plant and will be ready to harvest in about a month. Because of its quick-growing habit, keep a close eye on the plant to ensure it doesn't bolt (form flowers) before you have time to harvest it.

It also doesn't like constantly wet soil, so let the soil become fairly dry between waterings. Check daily, and, once the soil has become dry, water it immediately. Don't water it on a set schedule—stick your finger in the soil or use a water meter, and water when the plant needs it. This is *not* a plant for a self-watering or wicking container.

Because cilantro can be a little finicky and does not last more than a season even with the best of care, start a fresh pot of seeds every few months.

Growing Guidelines	Gentle morning sun/light, then part shade in the afternoon.
Fertilizer	Not needed until plant is mature, then use a high-nitrogen fertilizer at half strength every other week when actively growing.
Pests	Aphids
Diseases	Leaf spot, powdery mildew

Mint

To say that mint is easy to grow is an understatement—if you're not careful, it can be invasive. Grow all varieties of mint in their own pots or they will quickly take over and kill other plants. I've even had an errant mint send a stem into an adjoining pot and take root there.

The three basic types of mint are mint, peppermint, and spearmint, and there are several varieties within each of these types, such as chocolate, apple, and banana. All are quite hardy.

When your mint plant starts to become root-bound, you can simply cut sprigs to root into a new pot. Look for a long stem that has been touching the soil, and check each node (where the leaves meet the stem). If they've been in contact with the soil, you'll likely see small roots already forming. That's ideal, but even cutting a sprig and putting it horizontally in the soil should do the trick.

Although mint likes a lot of water, let the soil dry a bit in between waterings to prevent fungal diseases.

While mint is non-toxic to humans, ingesting large amounts can cause vomiting, diarrhea, and even liver damage in cats and dogs. Even though mint is used to repel insects, never rub mint leaves on your pet.

Growing Guidelines	Prefers part shade but will tolerate full sun/light and moist soil.
Fertilizer	None needed
Pests	Whitefly, spider mites, aphids, mealybugs (these are not usually a problem unless the plant is stressed)
Diseases	Rust (fungal disease)

Oregano

Oregano is a hardy perennial and looks similar to mint because it's a member of the same family. Some varieties of oregano are almost indistinguishable from mint, but a quick nibble of a leaf will reveal which it is. Other varieties have softer, fuzzier leaves, which make them easier to tell apart.

Although most plants start out growing close to the soil, they can grow up to 2' (61cm) in height. They are a Mediterranean herb that likes full sun and the soil a little drier, needing only medium moisture and very well-draining soil. The exception to the full sun rule is the golden oregano variety, which prefers partial shade so its leaves don't get sunburned.

Oregano actually does better if the soil is not too fertile, and, as we mentioned, it likes to be a little drier. If you're

Parsley

Parsley is not just for garnish! Fresh parsley, added at the end of cooking, imparts a wonderful flavor to a variety of savory dishes. Flat-leaf (Italian) parsley is the most common type used for cooking, but you can get the curly-leaved variety too. If you don't like the slight bitterness of the curly variety, stick with flat-leaf.

Parsley is very slow to germinate, and you might not see any signs of life for several weeks. It's best to stratify the seeds before planting—see the sidebar in Chapter 12 for directions (page 158). If you don't want to do this, soak the seeds overnight and plant them very close to the soil surface. Even if everything goes right, it will take about 14 weeks from planting to harvest. It's a good strategy to grow a new pot of parsley every month or two.

When you harvest parsley, cut a few stems close to soil level, which will encourage new growth, but don't harvest more than one-third of the plant at a time. If you really like parsley, have two pots going simultaneously.

Parsley is a biennial, so it will only last for one season if you want to eat it. In the second season you'll find that it's fairly bitter. Keep it growing longer if you want it to go to flower and collect seeds.

There aren't really pest problems for parsley grown indoors. When you grow it outside, the biggest "pest" is the black swallowtail butterfly. I'm happy to sacrifice my outdoor plants for those beauties and would even take my indoor pots outside during the right time of year to help.

Most disease problems can be avoided by harvesting leaves and using a fan for good air circulation.

Growing Guidelines	Full sun/light to part shade. Never allow the soil to dry out, but don't let the plant become waterlogged either.
Fertilizer	Half-strength vegetable fertilizer every six weeks
Pests	Not usually a problem
Diseases	Septoria leaf spot, flight, powdery mildew, damping off

making your own growing medium, use a little less compost and vermiculite and a little more peat moss or coco coir—more like the seed starter mix we featured on page 60.

You can start harvesting when the plant is just 4"–5" (10–13cm) tall. Cutting will stimulate the plant to produce more stems and result in a fuller plant. Oregano grows on woody stems, and you'll only use the leaves. The best way to remove leaves is to cut a long stem and hold the tip of the stem (uncut side) between the thumb and forefinger of your non-dominant hand. Then use the thumb and forefinger of your dominant hand to strip the leaves off the stem.

It's also a good idea to harvest stems all around the plant (don't just grab a handful of stems in one area), especially around the older growth in the center of the plant. This will

give the plant more air circulation, which will help prevent fungal problems.

Growing Guidelines	Seeds need light to germinate, so cover lightly with just a little soil and provide supplemental lighting.
Fertilizer	None needed
Pests	Aphids and spider mites
Diseases	Botrytis rot, rust

Rosemary

It's best to purchase an established rosemary plant rather than start from seeds. Seeds require stratification—see Chapter 12 (page 158) in order to have much chance for success. The next best option is by taking a cutting from a plant, but even that takes forever to grow. If you buy an established plant, you may want to start cuttings immediately to share with your friends. Once your seedling or cutting establishes roots in its new home, pinch the tip of the plant to encourage more branches to grow.

Once you've got your rosemary plant up and growing, it will be a terrific evergreen perennial shrub with a very pleasant scent. When grown outdoors, it can be 3'–5' (1–1.5m) tall and wide. You can keep it at a more manageable size indoors in a pot. If you want to keep your rosemary in a smaller pot, about 12" (31cm) in diameter, but it starts to become root-bound, you'll want to ease it out of the pot and trim the roots—a couple inches (about 5cm) all the way around—then return it to the pot with some fresh, well-draining growing medium. At this time, it's a good idea to take off some of the top growth.

Coming from the Mediterranean region, rosemary prefers sandy soil that doesn't have to be very nutritious, so the seed-starting mix in Chapter 6 (page 60) is good—you can even cut down on the amount of compost by half. Originating from a coastal area, rosemary needs full sun and good air circulation (imitating the constant sea breeze). It benefits from some supplemental lighting.

Only water when the soil is completely dry, but lightly mist the foliage with water several times a week (imitating sea spray). While it likes to be misted, it does not like to be kept in a too-humid environment, so also provide good air circulation.

Growing Guidelines	Full sun/light. Very well-draining soil.
Fertilizer	Once a year with fish/kelp emulsion
Pests	Aphids, spider mites
Diseases	Powdery mildew

Sage

We always think of sage being used for poultry dishes, especially our Thanksgiving turkey, but it's more versatile than that. Try it in any savory dish that can stand up to its earthy flavor. The grayish, wooly leaves are fun for those who like a tactile garden.

Depending on the variety, if you don't control the size, it can grow up to 2' (61cm) tall and 3' (91cm) wide, but there are shorter, compact varieties available. Harvesting actually encourages vertical growth. It's suggested to not harvest your plant until the first year to allow it to establish better. Thereafter, feel free to harvest at any time. Younger, smaller leaves on tender stems are more flavorful than larger ones that are on woody stems.

Even though it's a perennial, it will become woody and may only last four years or less. Explore different types like purple, golden, tricolor, and variegated varieties.

Growing Guidelines	Full sun/light. Drought-tolerant and doesn't like constantly wet soil.
Fertilizer	Doesn't need much—add a little compost halfway through the season.
Pests	Not really bothered by pests
Diseases	Various fungal diseases

Seasoning Celery

If you live in the United States, it's very likely that you've never heard of seasoning (cutting) celery. Unlike regular celery, the plant does not form thick stalks; instead, what you're after are the glossy, savory leaves that fan out from the plant and have a marvelous celery taste. The thin stalks can be chopped and used in soups and salads.

While these plants like full sun, you'll want to provide them with some light shade in the afternoon. Plant a few seeds no more than ¼" (0.6cm) deep about 8" (20cm) apart, and keep the seeds evenly moist. They'll take a while to show up, and germinate at different times, but they're worth the wait. When they are a few inches (about 7cm) tall, if you get more than four sprouts in a grouping, cut the others out.

For best flavor, keep the plant consistently watered. Plants can grow to 12" (31cm) in height. When you harvest, you can use the herbs fresh or tie a bunch together and hang them upside down in a cool, well-ventilated area.

Growing Guidelines	Full sun/light, but appreciates afternoon shade. Direct sow or start early planting ¼" (0.6cm) deep. Water regularly.
Fertilizer	High-nitrogen fertilizer monthly
Pests	Aphids
Diseases	Fungal blight

Thyme

Another Mediterranean herb is thyme, a woody perennial that grows low to the ground and loves drier soil and bright light. If you're growing thyme, it's basically a set-it-and-forget-it plant—it really doesn't like to be fussed over.

Different varieties of thyme have different growing requirements, so check the seed packet or plant label for more specific instructions. There are summer, winter, English, and French thymes, as well as citrusy lemon, lime, and orange thymes. Be careful, though—while there are around 400 varieties of thyme, only a few are good for culinary use, so be sure to choose carefully.

Unlike most herbs where you want to remove the flowers, it's been said that thyme has the best flavor just before the flower opens. Thyme grows well in a south-facing window.

Although leafing plants normally benefit from nitrogen, too much nitrogen causes rapid plant growth and poor flavor. Space your plants about 12" (31cm) apart.

Growing Guidelines	Full sun/light, very well-draining soil. Drought-tolerant, so only water about once every other week, sometimes once a month.
Fertilizer	Tolerates poor soils but benefits from a half-dose of a low-nitrogen fertilizer every six months
Pests	No pest problems
Diseases	Can develop root rot if the soil is not dry enough

Specialty Plants

Garlic

Although we've already established that garlic is technically a vegetable, it's used more like a spice, so I've included it here. Garlic is divided into two main types—hardneck and softneck. Hardnecks will grow indoors, but the bulbs will be a lot smaller. I found this out firsthand since I chose a variety that I'm familiar with growing outdoor here in Maryland.

Softneck garlic is the best choice for indoor growing because it doesn't need a period of cold like hardneck garlic does. If you can find them, other garlics like Asiatic and Turban varieties also do well in warm climates, so they will also do well indoors.

Garlic is an anomaly because it needs a lot of light but doesn't seem to grow very well in artificial light. You'll need a bright, sunny window with lots of direct natural light. Be patient—it will take about six months to harvest your garlic.

Even if your garlic doesn't form large bulbs indoors, you'll get plenty of great garlicky-flavored greens.

Unlike plants that grow from seed, garlic is grown from the individual cloves from a garlic bulb. Some people have grown garlic from a store-bought bulb, but it's better to get cloves from an online seed seller if you live in a colder climate where hardneck garlic is grown. The problem is, garlic is only available for sale at certain times of the year. Plant it as soon as it arrives.

Gently break the bulb apart into individual cloves and keep as much of the papery husk on as possible. The cloves should be firm, and you should discard any bulbs that are soft, as they will rot in the soil. Fill a pot to within 2" (5cm) of the top with a good growing medium. If your goal is just

WHAT MAKES A SPECIALTY PLANT?

I've included these four specialty plants in a separate section because they are grown differently—not from seeds, but instead from individual cloves of a garlic bulb (for garlic), rhizomes (for ginger/turmeric), and corms (for saffron crocus).

You're probably familiar with bulbs, but with garlic, you don't just plant the whole bulb (it's also called a head), but rather you grow it by breaking the bulb into individual cloves and planting the cloves separately.

Rhizomes are basically underground stems that grow horizontally in the soil. When they grow, rhizomes send shoots upward and roots downward. This is why you have to look at them and see which way to plant them in the ground.

Corms look like bulbs, but are more similar to rhizomes; they are round stems that grow underground.

to harvest garlic greens, plant several cloves fairly close in a small pot. If you want to harvest bulbs, then plant one clove per small pot, or 4"–6" (10–15cm) apart in a larger pot, with the tip of the clove pointing up. Cover with ½" (1.3cm) of soil and pat it down a bit. Water very slowly and gently, and cover with more soil if the water uncovers any of the cloves. Keep the soil moist but not wet.

If you are growing for greens, you can start snipping the leaves once they are about 2" (5cm) tall. Leave at least 1" (2.5cm) on the plant so it will continue to grow.

If you are growing bulbs, you must cure (dry) your garlic, or it will rot very quickly. Harvest the bulbs when about half the leaves of the plant are brown and dry. Braid or tie bunches together and hang them in a warm location, but not in direct sunlight. They'll do better if you have fans blowing on them—they may need several weeks to cure. Do not store them until they are completely dry and the outer skin is papery.

Garlic is very poisonous to dogs and cats and can cause red blood cell destruction. If your pet ingests garlic, contact a local emergency vet immediately, or call the National Animal Poison Control Center (1-800-548-2423) or the ASPCA's Animal Poison Control Center (1-888-426-4435).

Growing Guidelines	Push individual cloves into the soil and cover with ½" (1.3cm) of additional soil. Water well.
Fertilizer	When the leaves appear, use a high-nitrogen fertilizer
Pests	Thrips
Diseases	White rot fungus

Ginger and Turmeric

Since they're family members, you'll grow ginger and turmeric the same way, with the only major difference being how deep you plant them. Although ginger is commonly called ginger root, both plants are actually rhizomes, which are basically defined as modified underground stems that are able to produce both the shoots and roots of a plant.

Choose a container about 12" (31cm) wide and 12" (31cm) deep and fill it with a good growing medium. Choose rhizomes that look fresh and don't have wrinkled skin. Fill a bowl with warm water and let the rhizomes soak at least 8 hours.

Put a few firm, plump rhizomes that have several eye buds on them into the container with the eye buds facing up—that's where the shoots will form.

You can cut ginger and turmeric into smaller pieces if you'd like, but make sure they have at least three eye buds on each piece. Plant rhizomes about 6" (15cm) apart, cover with 2" (5cm) of soil, and water well. Place the pots in a warm area but not in direct sunlight. Be patient, because it can take months for the shoots to appear.

Mist the soil with a spray bottle daily, but don't overwater. After a couple weeks, you can use a watering can to gently water about twice a week instead of misting—let the soil dry before watering again. Use a water meter or stick your finger down 2" (5cm) into the soil to make sure it's dry before watering.

Once the leaves appear, if they turn yellow, it's a sign you're overwatering. Scorched leaves could be a sign that they're receiving too much direct light. If the leaf tips turn brown, it could be that you're adding too much compost (see below) or adding other fertilizers.

Once shoots have formed aboveground, wait several months and then check to see if the rhizomes have grown. You can remove it from the soil, cut off what you'd like, and replant the rest. So that you don't lose any valuable flesh, don't use a knife or vegetable peeler to take the skin off. Instead, use the side of a spoon to "peel" the skin off.

You can put ginger and turmeric in a zip-top bag in the freezer. Pull them out and use a grater when you need some for a recipe. Both ginger and turmeric make a delightful and healthy tea.

Growing Guidelines	Keep out of direct sunlight. Do not overwater.
Fertilizer	Add 1" (2.5cm) of rich compost on top each month and gently scratch it into the surface of the soil.
Pests	Aphids, scales, mealybugs
Diseases	Bacterial wilt, soft rot

Turmeric

Ginger

Saffron Crocus

If you love saffron, you know how wildly expensive it is. It's a no-brainer to grow it yourself, and it's shocking how simple it is. Saffron threads are the stigma of the saffron crocus plant.

Not just any crocus will do! Specifically buy the fall-blooming saffron crocus (*Crocus sativus*). You will likely have to purchase the corms online, and they will be shipped to you at the proper outdoor planting time (usually in late summer). They're perennials, so they'll come back for several years.

You need to have realistic expectations, though—it would take about 150 crocus bulbs to grow just 1 gram of saffron, since each crocus flower produces only three stigma, but you only use about ⅛ teaspoon of saffron in a batch of saffron rice—that's about the amount of threads you get from three or four crocus bulbs.

Choose a container about 12" (31cm) wide and 8" (20cm) deep and make sure it has very good drainage, since crocus don't like to be in constantly wet soil. Add soil and plant the corms about 2"–4" (5–10cm) deep and about 3"–4" (7–10cm) apart. A 12" (31cm) pot will hold five corms.

Crocus like 8–10 hours of light a day, so put the pot about 1'–2' (31–61cm) away from the window where they will get maximum light as the sun travels across the room. You can also use a mix of sunlight and grow lights.

Their normal dormant period is in the summer. When they die back, do not trim the leaves from the corms, stop watering, and keep the soil dry. Start watering again in late summer or early fall to wake them up.

Growing Guidelines	See above
Fertilizer	None needed
Pests	None
Diseases	Fungal diseases can be prevented by proper watering and air circulation

Seed Starting

Seed starting can be a fun activity for the whole family. If the weather allows, do it outside for the fresh air and less cleanup!

Buying Seeds

The way to save the most money in both your indoor and outdoor gardens is by starting your own seeds instead of buying transplants at the store. A packet of seeds is around $2 to $4, whereas buying transplants can cost $5 or more for a four-pack of small seedlings.

Another advantage is you'll find so many more varieties of seeds online than you'll find transplant varieties at the store. For example, the average big-box store will have five to ten varieties of tomato transplants, but I've seen upwards of seventy-seven varieties available both online and at special events I have attended.

As impressive as that is, it doesn't even begin to compare with the 650 varieties of heirloom tomato seeds available from *TomatoFest.com*.

Other than saving money and a wider selection of varieties, a third reason to start seeds is that when you're growing indoors out of season, it's impossible to purchase transplants. You'll never find tomato transplants at the garden center in the dead of winter. But that doesn't mean you can't have tomatoes while it's snowing outside!

You're probably thinking, Kim, there are twenty-five tomato seeds in that packet. I don't need that many plants. That might be true, but, properly stored, tomato seeds will last four or more years, and other seeds will last twenty years or more. How do you properly store seeds? It's simple. When you're done planting your seeds, fold over and tape the top of the envelopes, put them all into a large plastic zipper bag, throw in a couple silica (desiccant) packets, close the bag, and put it into your refrigerator. What's a silica packet? Those are those little "pillows" you find when you buy a new pair of shoes or a purse. Start saving them now, from the moment you read these words, and ask your friends and family to give you theirs. If you're in a bind, you can purchase silica packets online.

What most seeds need to start the germination process is moisture and warmth, which is withheld from them in your cool refrigerator and by the silica packets. There are a few that also need light to germinate, but they are rare, and that is also covered by your dark refrigerator. Oh, by the way, never put damp seed envelopes into the zipper bag, as they could start to mold.

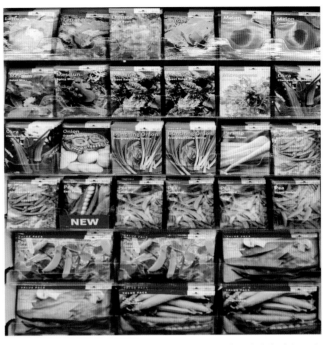

You can get some solid basics at a store, but remember that the Internet will have hundreds more options.

Before buying seeds, you need to decide what is important to you. Do they need to be non-GMO? Organic? Heirloom, open-pollinated, or hybrid? What varieties should you choose? If you don't know what varieties to look for, see Chapter 10 on choosing varieties based on their intended use. Read on for explanations of the different seed types I just mentioned to figure out which types will work for you.

GMO Seeds

Is having non-genetically modified organism, or non-GMO, seeds important to you? I mean, you don't want to grow something created in a laboratory, right? Would it surprise you to learn that home gardeners *cannot* buy GMO seeds? Even if you could, the price would be outrageous.

GMO seeds can only be sold in very large quantities to farmers who are generally required to sign a contract stating, among other things, that they will not resell them. Also, there are very few crops available where you can even find a GMO variety for sale. You'll see some of these in more than one category, but GMO crops include alfalfa and corn for animal feed and cotton for textiles. The ones for direct human consumption are sugar beets (for table sugar); corn

You can look for non-GMO labels like this one, but remember that no seeds sold to home gardeners are actually GMO seeds, so you can basically buy any seeds you want without having to worry about their GMO status.

If something is labeled USDA-certified organic, it may still have been treated with certain chemical fertilizers and pesticides.

(for corn syrup); canola, cottonseed, and corn (for oil); and papaya, soybeans, and squash (for food). Home gardeners would not ever want to purchase GMO seeds because they are so much more expensive than regular seeds—the cost only makes sense if you grow and sell the crops on a large scale.

You may be asking at this point why seed sellers stress that their seeds are non-GMO. The answer is marketing and consumer expectations. Vendors want to emphasize that their products are GMO-free, even though you can assume any seed sold to the general public is indeed GMO-free. I teach several small-space gardening methods, the most well-known being Square Foot Gardening. Because we use very few seeds in that course, I used to sell small quantities of heirloom seeds in tiny packets. People would pointedly tell me that they wouldn't purchase them because they weren't marked as non-GMO, thus they *must* be GMO. This simply isn't true.

Fighting for clean food and clear, truthful labeling of food and seeds is noble, but please don't penalize seed companies if they don't list their seeds as "non-GMO." If you have *any* concerns, just ask their customer service department for clarification. It's your right!

Organic Seeds

Since we're on the topic of myths, the next one is the use of the word "organic." We think we're making the best choices for our families by purchasing organic food. A 2019 article written by a nutritionist for *Good Housekeeping* magazine about the meaning of the word "organic" caught my attention because the subtitle was, "It's not a synonym for healthy, that's for sure."

We might think that seeds labeled as "organic" by the United States Department of Agriculture (USDA) would always come from plants that were not treated with *any* pesticides, fertilizers, or other chemicals. Hopefully that's the case, but it's simply not guaranteed. There are a very limited number of sanitizers, fertilizers, fungicides, and pesticides authorized by the USDA for use in organic agriculture. Be aware that what you think of as "organic" isn't necessarily the same as someone else's definition. This is another great reason to grow your own food.

Heirloom, Open-Pollinated, and Hybrid Seeds

Another decision you have to make regarding your seeds is if you want heirloom, open-pollinated, or hybrid seeds.

According to Seed Savers Exchange, "Heirloom varieties have a history of being passed down within a family or community. When seeds are gathered, they will breed true to the parent plant. All heirloom plants are open-pollinated, but not all open-pollinated plants are heirlooms." They continue, "Open-pollinated [plants] are

Heirloom seeds are great because they usually have a long history to them, and you can save seeds from the plants to grow them again or pass along to friends.

F1 seeds mean the seeds are hybrids. They're perfectly good choices for your home garden, but consider them once-and-done seeds: you won't be happy with the results if you collect and plant the seeds for a second generation.

plants that are pollinated by insects, birds, wind, humans, or other natural mechanisms. Heirloom and open-pollinated plants are more genetically diverse. As long as pollen is not shared between different varieties within the same species, then the seed produced will remain true to type year after year."

The advantage of heirloom and open-pollinated plants is that you only need to buy seeds once, grow them to maturity, and collect the seeds for use in subsequent seasons knowing that they will be the same as the parent plant. Collecting and processing seeds is different for each type of plant, and you can learn how to do so online at *SeedSavers.com*.

Now let's turn to hybrids. Have you ever picked up a transplant at the store or looked at a seed catalog and seen "F1" in the description? This is an abbreviation for "Filial 1" or "first child," and it indicates that the plant was deliberately created or bred for a particular trait such as disease resistance, shorter height, etc. While hybridization can, of course, happen in nature, the F1 seeds you buy are a result of controlled pollination. The goal is to make the plant more pest-resistant or produce larger, tastier, or faster-growing fruits. It's not worth saving seeds from hybrid plants, as you won't get what you're expecting.

Let's make our own pretend hybrid to illustrate. We love that Tomato A grows very quickly and is cold tolerant. Tomato B is resistant to a certain tomato disease, let's say

bacterial wilt, that's common in Tomato A. We hybridize them to form Tomato AB to produce a new breed that will grow quickly but resists bacterial wilt. If your hybrid is successful and the fruits are super yummy, you'd love to collect and plant seeds from your Tomato AB. However, the plants from these seeds will never be what you got from the original hybrid you bred. Some will show characteristics from Tomato A and some from Tomato B. They might even look like the original hybrid, but the taste will be off. Planting seeds you've collected from a hybrid is a roll of the dice.

Even though we've already established that you can't buy GMO seeds, let's talk about them for a moment, using a fun but wild example, and compare them to hybrids. Genetic modification introduces the DNA of a completely different species into the equation. A random example of this would be splicing the DNA of a salmon into the DNA of a tomato. Two different species and a laboratory are involved. Now, let's compare this to hybridization, which can be done by random pollination by a bee or by a plant breeder under more controlled conditions. The most relatable way to think of the hybridization process is to say we have two different breeds of dogs: a Schnauzer and a Poodle. If they mate, the resulting offspring would be a Schnoodle. These would be your F1 hybrids, and it happened through a natural process. Hopefully, now you won't be hesitant to purchase and use hybrid seeds and plants in your garden.

What Seeds Need

There are a few exceptions, but in general, the first two things seeds need to germinate are moisture and warmth. Once the plants pop up through the soil, they'll need light.

Seed Starting Equipment

When growing indoors, you can direct sow your seeds in their intended containers and should do so if the package directions say that it's best. I still prefer to grow many of my transplantable crops separately for a couple reasons. Although there are exceptions, seeds tend to germinate better in a growing medium with fewer nutrients than the soil you've chosen for your containers. Many seeds benefit from extra warmth provided by a heating mat, and a few need to be scattered on the soil surface and then require bright supplemental lighting to germinate. Look on the seed packet or online for the optimal way to start different types of seeds.

The essential tool you'll need is something in which to start your seeds. These can be purchased pots, flat seed trays, or containers you've saved, like pressed paper egg cartons, paper cups, and yogurt cups. Used pots and containers should be thoroughly scrubbed and disinfected to prevent disease by soaking in a 1:10 bleach to water solution for a few minutes, rinsed well, and allowed to air dry.

Most seeds get their best start in a fresh, soilless seed starting mix or fine vermiculite where there are fewer chances of disease problems than with regular potting or garden soil. See Chapter 6 for the seed starting mix recipe from Veteran Compost.

Commercially available seeding systems can easily be found in garden centers and online. If you're unsure, you

A heat tray can give the boost of warmth your seeds need to germinate and sprout quickly.

You can grow seedlings in individual pots or shallow plastic trays—sometimes called flats. You will need to buy different inserts—either drainage trays (shown here) or individual cells/packs.

can buy a seed starting kit with everything you need. The most common configuration is quite similar to the setup explained for soil-based microgreen kits in Chapter 9: a solid bottom tray to catch excess water and a drainage tray that holds the seed starting mix. There may be a clear plastic moisture dome in the kit to place on top of the drainage tray. Some fancy kits even have built-in heating. You can also buy heating mats to place under your starters.

Instead of a regular drainage tray, where you would have one large rectangle of soil, you can sometimes substitute "cell" trays, where the plants will already be in separate little cups that will make for easy planting down the line.

Ready-to-buy kits usually have thick plastic trays that last several years and are easy to carry from place to place. All these materials can also be purchased separately.

If you're looking for more eco-friendly options, you can use peat pots or coir pots. Some you'll need to fill with soil, while others you just place small "pucks" into water and they'll expand in size. One of my favorites is Cow Pots, made from recycled, composted cow manure—no, they don't smell. They are biodegradable and, once they are watered, last 12–16 weeks, which is plenty of time to grow the transplants. Just fill with your favorite soil, and as they grow, the cow manure gives your plants a boost of nitrogen, which helps young seedlings.

Another great option I've used for over a decade in my outdoor garden is the soil block system from Johnny's Selected Seeds. You start with small ¾" (2cm) cubes. When the plant outgrows this cube, you make successively larger cubes with divots in them that are the perfect size to just plop the smaller cube into it. You'll need to make or buy a special soil blend that's a bit stiffer than regular growing soil so the blocks hold together. Recipes to make your own soil block mix are available online. Search several sites to find the recipe you like best.

No matter what biodegradable pots or soil blocks you use, the benefit is that when you plant your seedlings in their final location, you're not disturbing the roots, which could result in transplant shock like they might experience when taking them out of plastic trays or cells.

Planting Your Seeds

Fill your trays or pots with moist seed starting mix. Never plant seeds or transplants in dry soil and wet it after, as most articles instruct. Otherwise, the dry soil surrounding the wet soil will pull moisture away from the seeds or plant roots. It's best to start with a consistently moist soil.

Plant your seeds to the depth recommended on the seed packet. Some seeds need to be planted 1" (2.5cm) deep, while others should just barely be sprinkled on top of the soil. One thing to ignore on the seed packet is how many

Cow Pots are an eco-friendly option made from cow manure—but don't worry, they don't smell.

Soil blocks can help prevent shock to the seedlings when they are replanted.

STRATIFICATION AND SCARIFICATION

When you research how to start your seeds, you might run across the terms *stratification* and *scarification*.

Some seeds require a period of cold and then warmth before you plant them. This is called stratification. Basically, you're mimicking a period of cold winter weather where the seeds go dormant, followed by warmth that triggers growth as it would in the spring.

This can be accomplished simply by placing moist sand or peat moss in a plastic bag with your seeds, zipping the bag shut, and storing them in the refrigerator for a certain amount of time. Some crops, like strawberries, don't like to be put in peat moss, so do your research for each type of seed. Instead of sand or peat moss, I like to use paper towels, as shown here. Be sure to label the paper towel and write the date you started them.

Stratification should be used specifically for perennials like strawberries, lavender, and rosemary that don't have good germination rates. If you notice, people usually grow their strawberries by ordering bare root plants, and rosemary and lavender propagate better from cuttings than from seeds. If you choose to grow from seed, stratification is highly recommended for better success.

After the period of time indicated on the seed packet, take them out of the refrigerator. You can either plant them right away or leave them in the bag and place it in a warm spot until they start to sprout. If you can't find the information, stratify your seeds for a minimum of two weeks.

Stratification How-To

1 Cut squares of paper towel that can be folded up like envelopes. Write the seed name on a folded-down top.

2 Place some seeds onto the paper towel below the area that will be folded down.

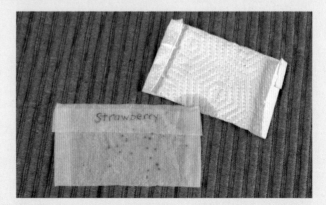

3 Fold the top back down, fold the sides, and moisten the "envelope" thoroughly.

4 Place in a zip-top bag and store in the refrigerator for the recommended amount of time.

Some seeds have exceptionally hard outer shells, which means they will need to go through the scarification process. In the wild, these hard-coated seeds would experience a period of freezing and thawing or pass through a bird or animal's digestive system, which weakens the hard outer coat.

To mimic these processes, you'll rub the individual seeds on sandpaper or use a nail file to thin out the hard shell so the seed can absorb water to germinate. Some people also nick them with a knife, razor blade, or toenail clippers, but I don't recommend this method, as it can be dangerous to you and you can easily cut into the soft inner seed, damaging it.

After you sandpaper the seeds, soak them in warm water for about twelve hours. When they've had the chance to absorb some of the water, plant them right away, or they may rot.

seeds should be planted. I love the strategy taught to me by my mentor, Mel Bartholomew, the creator of the Square Foot Gardening method. In his books, Mel tells us to "be stingy with seeds." Poke a planting hole to the proper depth and only put two or three seeds into each hole. If you broadcast many seeds, i.e., take a handful of seeds and toss them randomly over the soil, you will need to thin them to the proper spacing. This can result in damage to the growing roots. It's better to space the planting holes and use fewer seeds. If all three seeds come up, use scissors to cut the weaker two.

If the directions call for it, add a bit more seed starting soil on top of the seeds and gently pat the soil so the seeds come in contact with it. Label your seeds at time of planting, because you won't remember what you planted—trust me.

Use a clear moisture dome or lay a piece of plastic food wrap on top of the soil, then put the tray or pots somewhere warm. Most articles you read will tell you that the top of a refrigerator will work, but that information is outdated, since new refrigerators are more energy efficient and typically don't produce enough heat to warm the soil.

If it's warm enough in your house, you won't need supplemental heating for seed germination, but I like using a heating mat for more consistent warmth. Don't use a heating pad that's meant to be used on your body, as it's not made to be used in damp areas. Unless something is specifically designed for use around moisture, electricity and water don't mix!

Consulting the directions again, see if your seeds need a bright light in order to germinate. This is rare, but some

Always label the seeds right after you plant them—it's too easy to mix them up or forget what they are.

seeds won't germinate unless they receive bright light, although most seeds don't need light to germinate.

Check your seed trays a couple times a day to make sure the soil is moist. Gently mist the soil as needed and give the moisture dome or plastic wrap a few squirts too. Using a gentle mist instead of harshly spraying the soil ensures tiny seeds planted near the surface aren't disturbed. As soon as the plants start peeking out of the soil, remove the dome or plastic, or else they may start to mold. Only use plain water, without fertilizer in it. Use the strategies mentioned in Chapter 6 to minimize the amount of chlorine that's in the water.

This is also the time to move the trays to a strong light source like a bright window or, better yet, use supplemental lighting.

Supplemental Lighting for Seed Starts

While we talked about supplemental lighting in Chapter 4, here's a quick primer. Basically, when you're talking about grow lights for starting seeds, the only two things you need to look at are lumens and Kelvin.

Lumens are the brightness or intensity of the light. You're looking for lights that are 2,000 to 3,000 lumens. That's what stops seedlings from becoming "leggy," meaning when they grow tall and spindly with few leaves, searching for light. If you're growing tomato seedlings, though, check out the next subsection for a great tip.

The other important number for seed starting is Kelvin, which indicates the type of light. You want to get to 4100K to 6500K. Things to look at on the package

Since this is not a full-spectrum light, it is best suited for seed starting.

I got lucky with this sage transplant I purchased—there were two plants in one cell.

are words like "cool," "natural," and "daylight," and not "soft" or "warm."

Make sure to have an adjustable stand for the lights so they can be started really close to the seedlings and raised as the seedlings grow taller. Initially, your seed trays don't need light, just warmth, which might require a heat mat. But when the seeds start breaking ground, you'll start your lights just 1"–2" (2.5–5cm) away from the top of the trays.

Don't forget that your plants also need a period of dark, so only put the lights on your trays for about twelve hours a day.

Store extra seeds as noted on page 153 or they can be shared with friends and neighbors or taken to a seed swap.

Buying Transplants

If you've decided not to grow seeds at home and instead are purchasing juvenile plants from the garden center, inspect each plant before buying. Gently ease the plant no more than 1" (2.5cm) out of the container. If there is a lot of soil around the roots, that's perfect. If there are a lot of roots growing out of the bottom of the container, or more roots than soil, and the roots and soil seem hard, don't buy it—it's root-bound. Taking the plant all the way out could irreparably damage it, and that's not fair to the seller. You can get all the information you need by looking at just the top section.

A seed swap is a great, inexpensive way to diversify your seeds, get rid of your extras, and meet fellow gardeners.

or look for sponsorship to cover event costs. Many locations offer seminars by local garden speakers, have garden-related crafts, provide snacks, etc.

In addition to the fee, participants are asked to bring a minimum number of seed packets, either commercially purchased or from open-pollinated plants that they've grown and collected the seeds from. Seeds should be no more than two years old and have been properly stored to ensure freshness. If they're not in commercial packets, a reasonable number of seeds should be placed in small individual envelopes clearly labeled with the type, variety, and year collected.

At the event, tables are placed around the room according to type: annual flowers, perennial flowers, native flowers, etc. Vegetables are usually sorted by family: brassicas (cabbage), solanaceae (tomatoes), cucurbitaceae (squash), etc.

Participants typically are given an opportunity to look around the room so they know which seeds they want to get when their turn comes. There are several rounds, and the organizers determine how to select which groups of people go first (those with birthdays in January, those wearing a red shirt, etc.) in a particular round.

One of my favorite ways to pass along my extra seeds, or to try new varieties of seeds, is to attend a seed swap. Seed Swap Day was created by my friend, Kathy Jentz, the publisher of *Washington Gardener Magazine*, which covers the Washington, D.C., and Mid-Atlantic region. Officially, Seed Swap Day is the last Saturday in January, but individual event coordinators can have them any time of year.

Each swap is run independently, and the organizers decide if they will charge the participants a small fee

At the end, people may be able to trade directly with others. Perhaps the packet you choose has fifty seeds in it, and you only need twenty-five. Bring extra envelopes and a pen so you can split packets with others.

Check out *www.seedswapday.com* to see if a local swap is listed in your area. If not, maybe you can create your own. Just form a small committee and find a location with plenty of parking.

If your tomato plant is tall and "leggy," just remove the lower leaves and bury the stem. They will eventually grow new roots at the nodes.

Hairs on tomato plants are a defensive mechanism. The ones near nodes will turn into extra roots if they come in contact with moist soil, which helps the plant absorb nutrients.

Here's another thing to look out for: frequently, stores have very large plants with flowers or even fruits on them. Don't buy them! It's so much better to buy a smaller plant that has not spent too much time in a plastic pot. It will catch up quickly, don't worry. Bigger isn't always better.

Tomatoes: Bury Them up to Their Necks

Spindly, "leggy" plants aren't good unless you're talking about tomato plants that you're going to transplant. Then, it can actually be a good thing if they get a bit leggy. In most cases, when you're transplanting seedlings, you're told to plant them so that the soil level of the transplant matches the level of their new home. Tomatoes, however, are one of the few plants you can, and should, bury deeper when you repot them. Just remove any lower leaves, keeping at least the top three to five true leaves before you bury them up to their necks.

Why do you want to bury your tomatoes deep? Well, do you see all the little hairs on the stem? When the ones near the nodes, those "knobs" on the main stem, come in contact with moist soil, they'll form more roots. These extra roots will help anchor the plant in its container and also take up more nutrients, resulting in a healthier plant.

Of course, you don't have to plant your tomatoes like this, but it's usually beneficial to the plant and to your harvest.

PART 5

TIPS AND TROUBLE-SHOOTING

In this part of the book, we'll discuss things that can go wrong when gardening indoors. Inspect your plants frequently for any signs of distress: holes, spots, and discolored leaves could mean pests, diseases, lack of nutrients, or a watering problem. There are an astonishingly large variety of different pest and disease problems around the world, and too many variables with your crop choices, to be able to cover it all here, but these basics will give you the tools to spot and solve common problems.

There are many resources online to help you identify and treat pest, disease, and watering problems. My suggestion for research is your state's extension service if you're in the United States, or contact an agricultural college to see if they offer assistance if you're outside the country. When researching, look for reputable sources. I tend to look on *www.scholar.google.com* because most of them are science-based resources ending with .edu, which indicates a school of higher learning. Another strategy is to search for your specific crop: "tomato disease problems," "images of cucumber pests," etc.

Troubleshooting is an important part of gardening.

CHAPTER 13

Watering, Composting, and General Tips

Using smaller tools intended for houseplants is ideal for the indoor garden.

We're entering the last sections of this book, can you believe it? I could have easily called this chapter "The Miscellaneous Chapter," because we're going to cover a few diverse areas. I'm going to show you how to build a couple DIY self-watering containers. We'll talk about mulching, pinching, and pruning your plants to keep them healthier, and I'll give you tips on how to bring a plant that you've grown outside indoors if you'd like to extend its life. We'll also cover composting.

Overwatering and Underwatering

As we've learned, overwatering is usually a bigger problem than underwatering. When in doubt, stick your finger about 1"–2" (2.5–5cm) into the soil. If it's wet, don't water the plant, and check the next day. Better yet, invest in a meter that measures the moisture in the soil. I use a 3-in-1 meter that measures water, pH, and light.

Self-Watering or Wicking Containers

If you don't want to water your plants as frequently, self-watering, or wicking, containers are the way to go. There are several commercially available self-watering containers on the market. If your budget doesn't allow for them, you can easily make some using simple materials (see the next page).

Another advantage of self-watering containers is that you won't constantly be splashing water on the plant leaves, which could lead to some disease problems. Self-watering containers are best suited for plants that like consistent moisture. Research the water needs of the individual crop. If the instructions on the seed packet or transplant label say that plants need a period of dryness between waterings, be sure to allow the soil to dry out a good bit before watering again.

If you are the type of person who forgets to consistently water plants, set an alarm on your smartphone every other day to remind you to check. Because of the controlled indoor environment, you usually won't have to water daily like you would outdoors in the summer. But with drier indoor air in the winter, when using a fan for circulation, or when using

What caused this poor rosemary to die? It could have been either too little or too much water.

It's easy to turn a "square" 1-gallon (3.8L) water container and some wicking cord into a self-watering container.

DIY SELF-WATERING CONTAINERS

Simple DIY Self-Watering Container

This super-simple container will take some of the guesswork out of watering. After you've assembled it, simply water the plant; excess water will escape through the holes and become trapped between the layers and will get sucked into the soil as needed. You can scale this up with any plastic container, like 5-gallon (19L) buckets and even storage bins, as long as they are safe plastics. Just add proportionately more holes.

Materials

- Two equal-size containers where one will nest inside the other
- Plastic bottle cap or other durable item that will act as a spacer between the containers
- Drill or awl

Instructions

1 Drill holes. Drill two or three ⅜" (1cm) holes in the bottom of one container.

Wicking DIY Self-Watering Container

The small containers above are great for starting seedlings and growing microgreens, baby greens, and small plants. Now let's learn how to make something a little larger for things like herbs, lettuces, radishes, and even micro dwarf tomatoes. Like the other design, you'll water from the top and the excess will wick back up when the soil starts to dry.

Materials

- One-gallon square plastic jug
- Saw
- Scissors
- Wicking cord (or a couple strips of T-shirt material)

This larger container can hold a larger plant.

Instructions

1 Cut a starting line. Measure 4½" (11.5cm) from the bottom of the jug and use the saw to create a small cut in the plastic.

4 Add the plant. Fill with soil and plant seeds or transplants.

2 Nest the items. Drop the spacer into the second container (the one without holes). Put the cup with holes inside the solid cup.

3 Add the plant. Add moist soil and seeds or transplants.

2 Cut the jug. Use scissors to cut a level line all around the jug.

3 Assemble the container. Flip the top part of the jug upside down, thread the wicking material through the hole, and press it into the bottom part of the jug.

5 Water. Water the plant like you would normally. Excess water will become trapped in the bottom of the jug and be wicked up through the soil as needed through the wicking cord.

supplemental lighting, you will need to check on them, at a minimum, every other day. This is when a moisture meter comes in handy, as the top of the soil might look dry, but the soil farther down may still be well saturated.

If you're starting seeds in shallow seed trays, especially when using grow lights, you'll still need to check daily.

Mulching

A great way to conserve water is to add a layer of mulch on top of the growing medium in your containers. If you use natural materials from outdoors, like woodchips or shredded leaves, you'll want to sterilize them before using them, as they can contain insects or pathogens. Use the same methods found in Chapter 14.

You can use things like hydroponic clay balls, newspaper, thick felt material, glass marbles, gravel—really any good, clean material. This can have an aesthetic bonus, too!

Pinching and Pruning

If you're dealing with soft plant materials, you can use your thumb and forefinger to "pinch" the plant to remove some damaged leaves. If the stem is woody or a normally soft plant stem is large, use sharp pruners to remove excess vegetation.

If you are trimming more than one plant, sterilize the pruners when going from plant to plant. Keep a rag and a spray bottle or cup with a sterilizing solution handy.

The easiest thing to use for a sterilizing solution is a 70%–100% solution of isopropyl alcohol, which does not have to be diluted. Another common household item to use is liquid bleach, which needs to be diluted 1:9 with water. I don't recommend bleach, though, because it can ruin your tools and your flooring. Using other chemical household cleaners is not advised.

Pinching and pruning serve a number of vital purposes. Removing dead, sickly, or rotting plant material and getting it out of the growing area can halt the spread of disease. **Do not** put diseased plant material into your compost. Pruning can keep your plants compact if space is an issue, allows for better air circulation, and may even increase your yield. Check each of your crops to make sure they can be trimmed and how to do it properly.

When growing tomatoes, there's always a debate whether or not to pinch the sucker growth. I prefer to pinch the suckers and keep the growth to a single stem/vine. It decreases the yield, because you're basically removing parts of the plant that will eventually flower and produce fruit, but I feel that it results in a stronger plant and allows for more air circulation. However, do not pinch or prune determinate tomatoes; see Chapter 10.

Mulching is a great way to slow water evaporation.

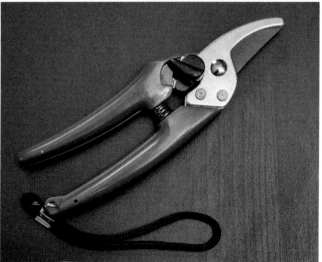

Pruners ensure you're making accurate, clean cuts that you sometimes can't get by just using your fingers.

To sucker, or not to sucker? Do what you feel is best for your tomatoes—I personally feel that removing the suckers will encourage strength in the plant.

Many plants can be brought in when it turns cold. Just make sure pests and diseases stay outside.

Bringing Outdoor Plants Indoors

If you want to continue to grow or just overwinter your prized outdoor plants, you'll want to closely inspect them for pest and disease problems before moving them indoors. Even before I did a lot of indoor gardening, I'd always bring in a tomato plant that was in a container.

When summer starts to fade, at least four weeks before you intend to bring in the plants, carefully inspect them one by one while they're still outside for evidence of pest problems like eggs, aphids, caterpillars, and worms. Depending on the type of pest, you should handpick them from the plant or use something like neem oil or insecticidal soap to get rid of the problem before bringing them inside. Identify the pest first and check online for the proper

remedy. For instance, with aphids, a blast of water knocks off the existing adults, but I'd follow up with a weekly outdoor application of neem oil or insecticidal soap. Inspect the plants again before bringing them in. If you spot any active pest problem, keep treating weekly.

If your plant is in the ground, you'll need to transplant them into a sanitized container with fresh or sterilized soil. If you're bringing in a plant already in a container, this is a great time to repot it. You'll want to also check for grubs or other pests that overwinter in the soil. See Chapter 14 for more information on pest problems.

At the same time, look for signs of diseased, dead, or dying plant material. Review the pruning information on the previous page on sterilizing your pruners when moving from plant to plant. See Chapter 14 for more information on disease problems. Cut away any dead twigs/branches and any leaves that show signs of insect damage. This way you have a clean slate and can tell if you have a new problem. Never bring a plant indoors that shows any signs of disease.

If these outdoor plants were grown in the ground or appear to be root-bound in their current container, place them into a larger sterilized pot with fresh, lighter, clean soil. Check online for each type of plant to see if you can remove it completely from the existing soil or if you should just put new soil around the existing root ball for less transplant shock.

If possible, isolate the moved plants in a separate area for a couple weeks indoors to make sure you don't spread disease or pest problems. Even if you don't isolate the plants, check carefully for any signs of pest or disease problems and take care of them right away.

Composting

Obviously, you won't have an open compost pile in your house, but there are a few indoor methods to consider. Think of how much material you have to compost in your home: garden trimmings, kitchen waste, newspaper, office paper, etc. It's not for everyone, but it is something that can be done.

With either of the two indoor methods described here, don't use any meat or dairy as ingredients. If you're using vermicomposting, buy your worms from a reputable vermicompost company and look for a complete list of what not to feed your worms.

What's wrong with this picture? Someone put obviously diseased material into their compost bin, which is not a good practice. It should be thrown into the trash.

No matter what method you choose, don't use any diseased plant matter in your compost. It's just not worth the risk.

Indoor Bin Composting

All this method takes is an opaque plastic or metal container with a tight-fitting lid. For instance, you can use a 5-gallon (19L) lidded bucket under the kitchen sink. For a larger bin, you could use an 18-gallon (69L) bin or metal trash can, placed in your indoor garden space or an easily accessible closet. You'll also need a waterproof tray with a lip at least 1" (2.5cm) tall. It needs to be somewhat larger than the compost bin, at least big enough to fit under the bin, to catch any liquid. Some suggestions are a round drip pan that goes under a water heater, a square pan for under a washing machine, or a rectangular rubber tray where you put your messy boots.

The type of composting you'll be doing here will be aerobic, meaning you need to have enough airflow into the bin to keep it from smelling. Drill a series of two or three dozen ¼" (0.6cm) holes in both the bottom of the compost bin *and* the lid.

Next, about 2" (5cm) down from the top of the bin, drill a row of holes horizontally around the circumference of the container. Drill another row of holes about 2" (5cm) below the first row. Set the bin on top of the tray, and you're ready to fill.

For composting, you'll usually have a desired ratio of browns, which are carbon sources like paper, cardboard, shredded leaves, etc., to greens, which are nitrogen sources like plant scraps. Unfortunately, you're usually told it should be something like 3:1 or 6:1. However, this is measuring the volume of the materials, not the actual volume of carbon and nitrogen within those materials. Finding the true amount of carbon and nitrogen is impossible.

So, take a deep belly breath in through the nose, hold it for a few seconds, and then exhale slowly out through the mouth. Relax—I don't want you to worry too much about browns and greens. Just add a few inches (about 7cm) of browns to the bottom of the compost bin, a very little bit of nitrogen-rich fertilizer, and then some greens. From that point on, just add browns and greens as you can find them.

The important thing is to have a good mixture of different ingredients and to chop them into small pieces. Make sure your compost is neither too wet nor too dry. If it's too wet, just add more dry browns like cardboard or shredded newspaper;

if it's too dry, moisten it and stir well. When you squeeze a handful of the mixed ingredients, it should feel like a damp sponge. If it begins to smell, you've got too much nitrogen and also need to stir in more browns.

Your compost is ready when it's dark brown and crumbly and you can't identify the ingredients. If it's almost ready, and you can still identify a few ingredients, just remove the good brown compost, leave the bits that haven't fully decomposed in the bin, and add fresh ingredients.

Vermicomposting

Vermicompost, a.k.a. worm castings or worm poop, is another easy indoor composting method. You can look online for instructions to create a simple DIY system from a couple opaque plastic bins. There are also commercially available vermicomposting systems. I found one that is simple to use that produces an abundance of rich compost. Fellow military veteran Steve Churchill from the Urban Worm Company has created a sturdy product called the Worm Bag. He was gracious enough to send me a sample.

No matter what system you use, you should take time to prepare the bin or bag according to instructions for your particular system before ordering the worms from a reputable company such as *www.urbanwormcompany.com*. What type of worms should you use? Steve says that while there are between 7,000 and 9,000 species of earthworms, only five to seven are truly suitable for vermicomposting. The top two he recommends are Red Wigglers (*Eisenia fetida*) and Indian Blue (*Perionyx excavatus*) worms. "They are epigeic, surface-feeding worms that process organic waste above the topsoil and in very loosely-packed material like leaf litter and manure," Steve explains.

Look what a great job worms do turning your kitchen scraps, garden waste, and shredded paper into valuable compost.

One of the best types of composting worm is the Red Wriggler.

CHAPTER 14

Pests, Critters, and Diseases

Add several yellow sticky traps in your containers as soon as you create your garden. They'll capture all sorts of flying insects that may have come in with your soil or plants. This will cut down on problems down the road.

Pest and critters and diseases . . . oh my! This is the chapter that everyone hopes they never have to use, but it is critical to become familiar with this information ahead of time so you can prevent, identify, and quickly solve whatever problem might arise.

Common Indoor Pests

Let's look at the most common pests that may bother your indoor plants. For each pest, I've recommended some solutions, but before applying anything, see the next section, Pest Treatments Explained, for more information about each treatment.

Aphids

These pests reproduce asexually, so they can quickly become a huge problem if you don't stay on top of it. The most common species of these pear-shaped pests are pale green, but they can be black, gray, white, and even pink. No matter what they look like, they can and will suck the life out of your plants. When a colony is well-established, a winged aphid may appear and fly to another plant to infect it.

Many times, aphids are found clustered on the stems of new growth, which will cause the leaves to look crinkled. If the infestation is bad, leaves will start to fall off the plant. These pests produce a sticky substance called honeydew, which attracts ants and the fungus that causes sooty mold.

To control aphids, you can squish them with your fingers, spray them with plain water, or, if possible, dip the foliage in a bucket of soapy water. You can also use insecticidal soap or a horticultural oil like neem oil. Because aphids reproduce so quickly, you will need to repeat treatments every week until the aphids are gone.

Spider Mites

These are hard to spot unless you've got a magnifying glass. Occasionally, you may see a tiny reddish dot crawling on your plant. If the infestation is bad, you will see clusters of spider mites underneath the leaves. They harm the plant by sucking the moisture out of the leaves. The first signs are usually very fine webs on the leaf tips or crunchy yellow spots on the leaves. Insecticidal soaps and horticultural oils will kill them immediately.

Scales/Mealybugs

For years, I thought scale was a plant disease, but they are actually a type of insect that suck the sap from plants. There are so many species of scale, and they can look quite different from each other. You may see them as brown ovals on your plant branches, white "cottony" growths on

Aphids

Spider mites

Scales/mealybugs

Fungus gnats

the leaves, or even waxy black, orange, or greenish bumps. Without treatment, leaves may turn yellow and fall off. With a heavy infestation, whole branches can die back. Like aphids, scales produce honeydew, which can attract ants and the fungus that causes sooty mold.

Scales can be either soft bodied or hard bodied, and once they latch onto the plant, they don't move, which makes them look more like a disease than an insect. They are hard to control and harder to treat. If the infestation is light, prune out any infested stems and dispose of them in the trash, not the compost pile. A cotton swab dipped in isopropyl alcohol rubbed on the scales will kill them, but the bodies will remain on the plant. This makes it difficult to tell if what you're seeing is a new, live scale bug or a dead one. Most of the time, it's simpler just to dispose of the entire plant early on to prevent the spread.

Fungus Gnats

Nothing's worse than having a swarm of gnats fly in your face when you're outdoors. Unfortunately, they are also a common problem indoors. The adults lay eggs on the surface of the soil, the larva burrow down to eat fungi and decaying plant matter, and the adults make their way to the surface to start the cycle over again. The problem is, when there's a large infestation, the larva can spread harmful pathogens and eat the plants' roots.

Fungus gnats are very small, gray/black in color, and have long legs. They look similar to tiny mosquitoes. While they do fly, it's more common to see them scurrying around on top of the soil.

As soon as I start growing indoors, I put up yellow sticky traps to catch them in several places—in pots and elsewhere around the growing area. Another way to kill

Fruit flies

them is to place a small, shallow container with equal parts of apple cider vinegar and water with a couple drops of dish soap stirred onto the soil in the planting pot. Because of evaporation, check daily to see if you need to refill the liquid. You can also use mosquito dunks, which are available in pellet form or as a donut. Fill a gallon jug with clean water, break up one-quarter of a mosquito dunk donut or use pellets, and place in the jug. Wait about twenty-four hours and use this to water the pots. If there is residue of dunks/pellets in the bottom of the jug, just add more water and let it sit. The Bacillus thuringiensis (Bt) in the dunks kills the larvae in the soil.

Fruit Flies

These beasties love the scent of ripe fruits, and you've probably seen them in your kitchen hovering around the fruit bowl. They won't be much of a problem until your plants start to fruit. The adults lay their eggs near the fruits; the fruits are the food source for the larvae, which appear a mere thirty hours after the eggs are laid.

The best solution is similar to the one discussed on the previous page for fungus gnats, but with an added step. Fill a small shallow container with equal parts of water and apple cider vinegar with a few drops of dish soap stirred in. Then add a cover of plastic wrap, aluminum foil, or a paper towel secured over the small container with a rubber band.

Poke several holes in whatever cover you've chosen. The hole has to be large enough for the adult fruit fly to enter; a toothpick works nicely. If you don't have a cover on it, the fruit flies will get a nice drink and simply fly off. With the cover, they'll be trapped in there and drown. You can also buy ready-made fruit fly traps.

Thrips

If you see stippled leaves or your blossoms die before they open, you may have Thysanoptera, a.k.a. thrips. They puncture the plants and suck out the contents, but at the same time, they can transmit viruses into the plant. Control them by using yellow or blue sticky traps, dusting with diatomaceous earth, or spraying with a horticultural oil solution containing neem oil.

Caterpillars and Worms

These creepie crawlies usually make it into the house when you bring a plant inside to overwinter or when you bring a transplant home from the garden center, so look at the underside of each leaf for eggs, caterpillars, and worms. Many times, these pests are similar in color to the foliage, so check carefully. To get rid of them, you can handpick them from the plants or spray them with a solution of no more than 2 oz. (60mL) of neem oil per 1 gallon (3.8L) of water. A Bt spray will also work.

Thrips

Caterpillars and worms

Pest Treatments Explained

Let's look a little closer at some of the treatment suggestions I made earlier. You'll notice that all of them are generally safe for humans and pets. When choosing commercially available products, I encourage you to use organic options.

Water

What could be simpler and safer than water? A mild infestation of aphids can usually be controlled with nothing more than a good squirt of water from a hand sprayer every few days. I suggest agitating the water and allowing some of the chlorine to dissipate for twenty-four hours before using, or running the water through a filter that removes chlorine. Check the list of what your filter removes.

Dish Soap

Many times you'll see liquid dish soap used in homemade bug sprays, but be careful. While they can kill many soft-bodied bugs, they can also harm some plant foliage. This is a case of more is not better. Use about 2 tablespoons (30mL) of dish soap per 1 gallon (3.8L) of water. Test the spray on a single leaf and let it sit for a couple hours. If you don't see any signs of distress, you can use it on the whole plant. Test on each and every crop where you intend to use the spray.

Insecticidal Soaps

Of course, the dish soap solution mentioned in the previous section could be considered an insecticidal soap, but there are many commercially available options. They usually contain potassium salts of fatty acids, commonly called soap salts, which penetrate the insect body, causing dehydration. They are used as insecticides, fungicides, algaecides, and herbicides. Yes, you read correctly—herbicides. A few plants can be sensitive to insecticidal soaps, so test a single leaf on each crop and look for signs of distress after a few hours before using it on the entire plant. Bean and cucumber plants are especially sensitive.

Horticultural Oils

Horticultural oils, such as neem oil or mineral oil-based products, can be handy if you catch the problem early. They can be purchased as a ready-to-use spray or as a concentrate. Be sure to dilute them as directed and check the label, as some plants are sensitive to some oils. This is quite important—once, I used a too-strong solution and stunted some of my tatsoi plants. As with the soaps mentioned on the right, test a single leaf from each crop before using an oil on the entire plant.

Simply water can be a treatment for certain infestations.

Dish soap can be a handy treatment tool that you already have in your home.

Commercially available insecticidal soaps can offer stronger treatment.

Horticultural oils are best for the early stages of a problem.

When using diatomaceous earth, be sure it's labeled "food grade." It will be safe for humans and pets.

You can use bacteria to fight pests!

Food-Grade Diatomaceous Earth (DE)

Diatomaceous earth is made from fossilized algae-like plants called diatoms. The deposits of diatomite are mined, then ground into a fine, chalky powder. If you choose to use diatomaceous earth (DE), make sure it's labeled "food grade" on the package and is not the type used in swimming pool filters. Food-grade DE is great because there's no worry if a child or pet accidentally ingests a little. DE has microscopic sharp edges that cut the bodies of many soft-bodied pests, which dries them out. It doesn't seem to harm beneficial worms and soil microorganisms.

Caution: Wear a face mask over your nose and mouth when applying this fine powder. It can also be applied as a solution with a spray bottle. Use 1 cup (235mL) of DE to ½ gallon (2L) of water. Stir or shake frequently to keep the solution well mixed.

Bacillus thuringiensis (Bt)

Bacillus thuringiensis, more commonly known as Bt, is a natural, beneficial, soil-borne bacteria that is widely used for natural insect control. Different strains take care of bugs in different ways.

Bacillus thuringiensis var. *kurstaki* (Bt-k) is used for leaf-eating worms and caterpillars, while *Bacillus thuringiensis* var. *israelensis* (Bt-i) is found in mosquito dunks to take care of fungus gnat larvae.

Best of all, Bt is harmless to humans and other mammals, birds, and fish.

Yellow Sticky Traps

These are great for any flying insects. I put them in pots and containers all around my indoor garden from the moment I bring soil into the house; I have even found cute butterfly- and flower-shaped sticky traps online.

Other Natural Treatments

You've probably seen homemade pest control recipes using garlic or hot peppers. I don't like using them indoors in a small space because of the smell and volatile oils. I've heard

A simple sticky trap can be highly effective.

The benefits of other natural treatments, like garlic, are questionable, but you can experiment with them if you are willing to take the risk.

they might keep your furry friends and foes away from your growing area, though. Use any of these methods with caution and understanding that you may end up sacrificing a plant for the sake of your experimentation.

Critters

We love our fur babies, but it's frustrating when they destroy our plants. There is a greater chance of your pets being harmed by your regular houseplants than your edible plants, but there are some warnings worth noting.

My two "wombmate" rescue dogs, Jake and Carly, love to eat compost, blood meal, and bone meal, and I'm sure cats might find some of those delicious too. While they're not generally harmful if ingested in small doses, it's best to keep these products well away from your dogs.

Some common things you might grow that dogs and cats shouldn't have are members of the onion family, including scallions, shallots, and garlic. While ripe tomatoes won't hurt cats and dogs, they should only eat small amounts, and they should never eat any other parts of the tomato plant.

Of course, you should have the number of a local emergency veterinarian handy at all times. If there's evidence that your pet has eaten something, and you can't call a local vet, try the National Animal Poison Control Center (NAPPC) at the University of Illinois at 1-800-548-2423. Another option is the ASPCA's Animal Poison Control Center (APCC) at 1-888-426-4435 in the United States. Both of these resources will charge a fee for their service.

Before calling either service, be ready with your pet's species (dog, cat, etc.), breed (Poodle, Himilayan, mixed breed, etc.), sex, approximate weight, what type of plant was eaten, how much (if you know), and the symptoms. Have your name and credit card handy.

Obviously, the best solution is to keep your pets out of your growing areas completely, with physical barriers like a closed door. That's not always feasible, especially if your garden is in a public space in your home. There are devices with battery-powered motion sensors that will spray an environmentally-friendly deterrent spray when your animal approaches. It's odorless and won't harm surfaces, but you'll need to be strategic when placing it so you don't trigger the device every time you walk by.

In addition, your cat might want to use your larger containers as a litterbox. Putting an unpleasant-feeling mulch on top of the soil should do the trick. Cats don't like the scent of citrus, so you can put citrus peels in small mesh bags around your growing area. I've heard that citrus, rosemary, or tea tree essential oils will do the trick, but I don't have a cat, so I couldn't try it myself. Just a drop on a damp cotton ball at the entrance to your

Keep your plants safe from your pets, but also keep your pets safe from your plants.

growing area should be enough, but you'll need to refresh them often.

Mice and other rodents can also cause problems if you've already got them in your house. They'll dig up freshly planted seeds, and if you don't have your seed packets stored in the refrigerator or other rodent-proof container, they'll quickly find your seed stash and munch on them. To take care of a mouse problem, I don't recommend poisons, especially if you have children or pets in your house. They can be harmed if they find the poison. Your pets can be harmed if they eat a dead mouse that's been poisoned, and, if the mouse gets outside before dying, predatory mammals and birds could also be harmed from ingesting it.

If you're squeamish, you can use live traps and relocate the rodents. If not, then there are several types of kill traps. Be sure to put them somewhere children or pets can't access them. It's worth trying plug-in ultrasonic pest repellents. Read the reviews online to select the best for your situation.

Diseases

Different diseases bother different crops, the causes can vary drastically, and sometimes the symptoms are the same as a pest problem or improper watering, so we're not going to delve too deeply into diseases in this book. Rather, I'll help you look for resources that will allow you identify and solve your particular disease problems.

In Chapter 10, we talked about creating a garden journal. An important part of the information you need to collect in that journal is to note which pests and diseases can potentially bother each different crop. If you do this, it will certainly make it quicker and easier to identify and treat each problem as soon as it springs up.

While we're not going to go into the numerous disease problems that could potentially pop up in your indoor garden in detail, we'll talk about good practices to prevent most of these problems before they happen.

Here are three common causes of disease that you should strive to avoid.

- **Improper watering:** Improper watering is the most common reason for fungal disease and root rot.

If you see something strange on your plants, do an online search using the plant name—like "cucumber disease identification."

Unless your crop specifically likes its leaves wet, only water the soil. Never overwater your plants.
- **Bad air circulation:** Ensure your room has proper ventilation and air movement. Pruning plants and spacing them far enough apart also helps.
- **Improper fertilizer:** Apply the proper types of fertilizers based on your plants' needs, and follow the guidance on the package or on the seed packet as far as strength and frequency. This is definitely a case where the warning, "If little is good, more is not better," should be heeded. An underfertilized or overfertilized plant will be weaker, and a weaker plant will be more susceptible to diseases.

If you use good, new growing medium, weeds should not be a big problem. Be aware of where you plant your seeds, and remove anything that's out of place or consult an online weed identification guide.

You can use a pressure cooker or multi-cooker to sterilize soil.

Weeds

You should not experience weeds if you are growing in 100% compost, if it's been done correctly, or if you are using a brand-new bag of sterile growing medium. Correctly made compost has been brought up to 131–170°F (55–77°C) for at least three days. While you can grow in 100% compost, it's not a great solution for gardening in general and indoor gardening in particular. It's heavy and compacts easily, which can cause the loss of needed air space.

There won't be any weeds in your hydroponic system either unless there are weed seeds in your seed packet, which is not likely to happen.

I prefer to buy new, clean bagged soil rather than have to sterilize soil. If you brought soil or previously used growing medium in from outside, then it's quite likely that you will have problems with weeds unless you sterilize it before bringing it in.

If you should get weeds, just hand pull them as soon as they appear. If you're direct sowing seeds in a soil-based container, plant your seeds in strategic locations (i.e., in the center of the container for larger crops or in a noticeable pattern for smaller crops) so that you can instantly identify the young sprout as either a desirable plant or a weed.

Let's look at three methods for sterilizing soil to prevent weeds. In addition to killing weed seeds, added benefits are that sterilizing your soil will also kill most pests, nematodes, and disease-causing bacteria and viruses. The downside is that it will also kill beneficial microbes.

Steaming Method

Pour about 1" (2.5cm) or more of water into the bottom of a pressure cooker or multi-cooker. Add a wire rack. Put soil into a suitable-sized pan and cover with aluminum foil on the rack. Snugly attach the lid, leave the pressure valve in the open position, and turn it on. Once steam starts to escape, you know it's ready to start timing. Allow the pot to continue to boil, steaming the soil for thirty to forty minutes, then turn the pressure cooker off. Allow the soil to completely cool before removing it from the cooker. Transfer the cooled soil to a container with a lid or to a heavy-duty bag (i.e., contractor-grade trash bag or sandbag) and close tightly until ready to use.

It's *very* important that you keep the pressure valve in the open position. In this case, the goal is to produce steam, not cook the soil.

Oven Method

Preheat your oven to 180–200°F (82–93°C). Line a dedicated oven-safe container such as a metal or glass baking pan with aluminum foil, and add the soil. Cover it with more foil and put a dedicated oven thermometer (that you won't use in

An oven can do the trick to sterilize your soil as well.

If you want to reserve your oven and pressure cooker for food use only, try the outdoor solarization method.

food) into the soil toward the middle of the pan. Place the pan into the oven for a minimum of thirty minutes, until the soil temperature reaches 180°F (82°C). Do not let the soil get hotter than this. Allow the soil to cool and transfer it into a container with a lid or tightly closed bag until ready to use.

Outdoor Solarization Method

Personally, the ick factor of using something in which I cook food to process soil is just too much for me. The only method I'd personally consider is outdoor solarization. The process of solarizing is simple, but the downside is that this process takes several weeks, so you'll need to plan ahead.

Just take some lightweight soil/growing medium that you may have previously used in containers, put it into clear plastic trash bags, wet the soil well, close the bag, and leave it out in the sun for at least four weeks. If you can't find clear bags, use any other color and leave it an extra week. No matter the color, the bag will likely disintegrate, so transfer the soil into buckets to bring into the house.

Alternately, if you have good lightweight soil/growing medium in an outdoor raised bed, you can dampen the soil and cover the entire bed with plastic sheeting. This time, you'll use clear plastic instead of dark, and again it will take four weeks. Remove the plastic sheeting, and bring the soil into the house.

Resources

All information presented here was current at the time of writing. As we all know, stuff happens. Feel free to contact me at SFGKimRoman@yahoo.com for more information. You can also join me on Facebook or on Instagram @yourindoorfoodgarden. And I'd love to see you in one of my small-space veggie gardening classes; sign up at www.sfg4u.com.

Animal Emergencies

ASPCA's Animal Poison Control Center (APCC) (1-888-426-4435)
National Animal Poison Control Center (NAPPC) at the University of Illinois (1-800-548-2423): Keep this phone number handy in case your fur babies eat any indoor or outdoor plant or even start acting sick if they have ingested a food they shouldn't have. Have your pet's species (cat, dog, etc.), breed (Poodle, Himalayan, etc.), age, approximate weight, what it ate, and the amount (if known) handy. They'll also need your name and credit card number.

Composting

Urban Worm Company (*www.UrbanWormCompany.com*): Check out their selection of worm bags, composting worms, soils, and accessories.

Veteran Compost, Aberdeen, Maryland (*www.VeteranCompost.com*): Veteran Compost offers a variety of composts and soils available for pickup or local delivery. Some of their products like vermicompost (worm poop) and biochar can be shipped in the U.S. They are a veteran-owned business.

Containers and Growing Systems

AeroGarden (*www.AeroGarden.com*): AeroGarden has hydroponic systems from 3 to 24 plants with integrated full-spectrum grow lights. WiFi connectivity and an Internet app are available with some of the systems.

Click and Grow (*www.ClickAndGrow.com*): "Grow nutritious produce at home as easily as making your morning cup of coffee—add pods, add water, plug in, enjoy." Hydroponic systems are available that hold from 3–51 plants, all with integrated LED lights and a growing app. International shipping available.

Garden Tower Project (*www.GardenTowerProject.com*): This soil-based system will hold at least 50 plants in a small 30" (76cm) footprint. Turns 360 degrees and features a composting tube. Optional vertical lighting kit is suggested when growing indoors.

Hamama (*www.Hamama.com*): Super easy microgreen growing system—great for children or those with limited mobility. Unlike other microgreen growing methods, you don't have to test the water pH.

Rise Gardens (*www.risegardens.com*): WiFi-enabled and app-controlled tabletop and freestanding hydroponic systems with integrated broad-spectrum LED lights. The app tells you when to add nutrients or water, manages the lights, and tracks the progress of your plants so you know when to harvest.

Education, Information, and Services

City-Hydro (*www.City-Hydro.com*): "Top of the line microgreens growing supplies and free training." Sturdy food-safe plastic trays with a lifetime warranty. LED lights have a 50,000++ guarantee. Free unlimited online training for the PURE method using no fertilizers, no pesticides, no soil, and using pure H_2O.

Dwarf Tomato Project (*www.dwarftomatoproject.net*): "Community driven and delicious, The Dwarf Tomato Project has been going (and growing) for over 10 years with growers participating all around the world." Their goal is to create low-maintenance tomatoes of all flavor and size variations on compact, easy-to-maintain dwarf tomato plants. Seeds available for both the Northern and Southern Hemispheres.

Espoma (*www.espoma.com*): Great line of organic fertilizers and information about fertilizing your garden.

Fast Growing Trees (*www.fast-growing-trees.com*): Wonderful selection of dwarf and patio fruit trees and bushes.

The Garden of Words (*www.TheGardenOfWords.com*): Offering website services, business development & branding, and email marketing.

Seed Savers Exchange (*www.SeedSavers.org*): "The Exchange works to keep biodiversity strong and garden traditions thriving." Find and share heirloom seeds and browse their extensive education resources on all aspect of gardening and seed saving.

Seed Swap Day (*www.SeedSwapDay.com*): Check here to see if there's a seed swap location near you, or consider hosting one of your own and listing it on the Seed Swap Day website. While traditionally held the last Saturday of January every year, swaps take place throughout the year. Many sites feature guest speakers and fun crafts. #SeedSwapDay

Shawna Coronado (*www.ShawnaCoronado.com*): Author Shawna Coronado is best known for her creative methods of gardening; her goal is "empowering wellness through anti-inflammatory food, therapeutic gardening, and daily movement."

Square Foot Gardening 4 U (*www.SFG4U.com*): Kim helps you "Confidently Grow Your Own Food!" through online, on-demand small-space gardening classes on a variety of subjects such as Square Foot Gardening, vertical gardening, fall and winter gardening without a greenhouse, and more, along with virtual garden consultations.

Square Foot Gardening Foundation (*www.SquareFootGardening.org*): Interested in learning more about Mel Bartholomew's famous Square Foot Gardening method and/or becoming a SFG Certified Instructor? Great SFG resources and newsletter/blog information. Get involved in the mission of SFG, which is to "end world hunger, one square foot at a time."

TomatoFest (*www.TomatoFest.com*): "TomatoFest® is your ultimate destination for finding the best tasting, old-fashioned, and rare heirloom tomato varieties originating from many different regions and family farms, around the world. Our mission is to sustain these precious heirloom tomatoes, and their family and plant histories, so they may remain a vital and available food source for generations to come. We treat these heirloom tomato seeds as our precious legacy." Over 650 varieties of tomatoes and other vegetable seeds are available.

Valley View Farms, Cockeysville, Maryland (*www.ValleyViewFarms.com*): A great independent garden center, locally owned and operated since 1962, known for their helpful and knowledgeable staff and their annual events such as the Tomato Tornado.

Washington Gardener Magazine (*www.washingtongardener.blogspot.com*): A delightful publication serving Washington, D.C., Maryland, and Virginia-area gardeners, but much of the content is pertinent to edible and ornamental gardeners everywhere. Also look for Kathy Jentz's GardenDC podcast on your favorite platform.

Lights

Maxsisun (*www.Maxsisun.com*): Manufacturer of full-spectrum grow lights since 2009. Optimal plant growth and higher yields with less energy consumption to minimize production costs.

Seeds and Seed Starting

Baker Creek Heirloom Seeds (*www.RareSeeds.com*): Purveyor of unusual and rare organic heirloom seeds from all over the world. Their mission is to provide the seeds of a sustainable food supply for everyone and keep heirloom varieties alive for future generations.

CowPots (*www.CowPots.com*): CowPots exports excess nutrients from their sustainable farm to where they're needed (your garden) and replaces non-renewable planting containers like plastic and peat.

Johnny's Selected Seeds (*www.JohnnySeeds.com*): Johnny's Selected Seeds provides a large selection of seeds, tools, and educational resources for gardeners and farmers. Their focus is "helping growers succeed by developing tools that provide timesaving, labor-reducing solutions."

MI Gardener (*www.MIGardener.com*): Good source for reasonably-priced seeds and bare-root strawberry. Great resource for gardening knowledge. "MI Gardener strives to provide premium, free information for everyone, everywhere. Helping you grow food more efficiently, live a healthier life, and have fun doing it."

Renee's Garden Seeds (*www.ReneesGarden.com*): Renee Shepherd personally selects "heirloom and brand-new vegetables and herbs chosen for flavor and productivity and flowers chosen for their beauty, sustainability, and garden performance. Our packets feature detailed growing directions, harvesting tips, and cooking ideas. We offer both new and experienced gardeners satisfying success with seeds."

True Leaf Market (*www.TrueLeafMarket.com*): "Since 1974, True Leaf Market's brands, Mountain Valley Seed and Handy Pantry, have been providing a multitude of high-quality seed to residential and professional growers alike, which include flowers, vegetables, grasses, herbs, sprouting, long-term storage, and wildflowers. As an independent seed company, we've been thrilled to hear the feedback we get from our customers about their stellar results with their seeds. We hope to build and rebuild communities through growing by making gardening an accessible practice for all."

About the Author

Kim Roman is an Air Force veteran and has taught various methods of small-space, high-intensive vegetable and herb gardening since 2010. Her goal is to help people confidently grow their own food, and thousands of her students have done just that through both her in-person classes, online on-demand video offerings, and consultations.

She has been a Square Foot Gardening Certified Instructor since 2010, mentored by well-known author and creator of the SFG method, Mel Bartholomew. In 2019, she was bestowed the title of Square Foot Gardening Foundation Ambassador.

Her seminars and workshops are in demand at home and garden shows, garden clubs, and Master Gardener programs. She is an adjunct faculty member at Anne Arundel Community College in Maryland. One of her favorite activities is teaching staff and client "lunch and learns" at various corporations such as Johns Hopkins University, Northrup Grumman, Deloit, and others.

In addition, Kim's passion is to serve organizations that assist the homeless, work with at-risk youth, support wounded veterans, and help those living in food deserts. She believes that everyone is entitled to good, nutritious food, and, in 2018, taught gardening and composting classes in Kenya. She is a garden teacher, writer, speaker, and dabbles in photography. Her online classes are available at *www.sfg4u.com.*

Photo Credits

Key: KR = Kim Roman; CRP = Crystal Roman Photography; (S) = Shutterstock.com; fc = front cover; bc = back cover; t = top; b = bottom; m = middle; l = left; r = right; 2r = second row; 3r = third row; 4r = fourth row

fc 1r: FotoHelin (S); fc 2rl: ajborges (S); fc 2rr: CC7 (S); fc 3rl: Baker Creek Heirloom Seeds/RareSeeds.com; fc 3rr: Milaspage (S); bc background: KR; bc t: ClickAndGrow.com; bc ml: Andreas Chrysomallis; bc mr: CRP; bc b: Lilkin (S); 2: Kimberly Boyles (S); 4: N_Sakarin (S); 5 (and throughout) vine: NikhomTreeVector (S); 7 tl: Baker Creek Heirloom Seeds/RareSeeds.com; 7 tr: Baker Creek Heirloom Seeds/RareSeeds.com; 7 2rl: PosiNote (S); 7 3rl: Baker Creek Heirloom Seeds/RareSeeds.com; 7 2rm: CRP; 7 2rr: Baker Creek Heirloom Seeds/RareSeeds.com; 7 3rr: KR; 7 4rl: CRP; 7 4rm: CRP; 7 bl: Baker Creek Heirloom Seeds/RareSeeds.com; 7 br: KR; 10 all: Tessa Agrey; 11 all: Plant4Table; 12 all: Celie Brayson; 13 all: Andreas Chrysomallis; 14 all: Christopher Tsambis; 15 t: Jessica Doyle; 15 b: Eilidh McKnight; 16 all: Tatiana Serdyuk; 17 all: Dhanya Venugopal; 18 all: Emily Kichler; 19 all: Lorna Kring; 20–21: CRP; 22 (and throughout) leaf icon: Andy Dean Photography (S); 22: Guy DiRoma Photography; 23: Sirinn3249 (S); 24: KR; 25: Kuznetsov Dmitriy (S); 26: KR; 27: CRP; 30: CRP; 31 t: CRP; 31 bl: CRP; 31 br: baranq (S); 32: CRP; 33: CRP; 34 l: CRP; 34 r: CC7 (S); 35 t: KR; 35 b: KR; 36: yanin kongurai (S); 37 l: Aiempp147 (S); 37 r: Timothy Roman; 38 bl: Timothy Roman; 38 tr: KR; 38 br: KR; 39 tl: CRP; 39 tm: Timothy Roman; 39 tr: Timothy Roman; 39 b: KR; 40–41: Okrasiuk (S); 42: alexkich (S); 43 t: BNMK 0819 (S); 43 b: CRP; 44 t: CRP; 44 bl: CRP; 44 br: CRP; 45 l: CRP; 45 r: CRP; 46: asharkyu (S); 47 l: KR; 47 r: KR; 48: KR; 49: KR; 50: lilac 5 (S); 51 l: KR; 51 r: KR; 52 l: KR; 52 r: Aybarskr (S); 53: CRP; 54 l: Paul Maguire (S); 54 r: PattyPhoto (S); 56: KR; 57 l: CRP; 57 r: CRP; 58 t: KR; 58 b: FotoHelin (S); 60: KR; 61 l: CRP; 61 r: New Africa (S); 62 t: CRP; 62 b: Simone Hu (S); 63 t: Olya Maximenko (S); 63 m: Dan Gabriel Atanasie (S); 63 b: Niraelanor (S); 64 l: Ashley-Belle Burns (S); 64 r: VH-studio (S); 65: ViktoriaIvanets (S); 66: Gummy Bear (S); 67 l: CRP; 67 r: eurobanks (S); 68–69: CRP; 70: KR; 71 t: CRP; 71 b: KR; 72: Tribalium (S); 73 tl: Rosamar (S); 73 tr: Scisetti Alfio (S); 73 b: CRP; 74: Africa Studio (S); 75 bl: CRP; 75 tr: KR; 75 br: KR; 76 l: CRP; 76 r: KR; 77: CRP; 78: Floki (S); 79 tl: Alex_Traksel (S); 79 tr: N_Sakarin (S); 79 bl: Image Picker (S); 79 br: Sura Nualpradid (S); 80: Lilkin (S); 81 tl: Sura Nualpradid (S); 81 tr: Cergios (S); 81 b: Photo Win1 (S); 82–83 all: CRP; 84 tl: ClickAndGrow.com; 84 tr: AeroGarden.com; 85 l: CRP; 85 m: CRP; 85 r: CRP; 86: CRP; 87 t: KR; 87 b: KR; 88: ajborges (S); 89 l: KR; 89 r: Timothy Roman; 90 l: KR; 90 r: Bogdan Wankowicz (S); 91 tl: KR; 91 tr: CRP; 91 bl: KR; 91 br: CRP; 92 l: CRP; 92 r: CRP; 93 t: KR; 93 bl: Jordan Freytag, True Leaf Market; 93 br: Jordan Freytag, True Leaf Market; 94 t: KR; 94 m: KR; 94 b: KR; 95 t: Varavin88 (S); 94 b: CRP; 96–97: Baker Creek Heirloom Seeds/RareSeeds.com; 98: KR; 99: KR; 100: KR; 101 all: Baker Creek Heirloom Seeds/RareSeeds.com; 102 all: Baker Creek Heirloom Seeds/RareSeeds.com; 103 all: Baker Creek Heirloom Seeds/RareSeeds.com; 104 all: Baker Creek Heirloom Seeds/RareSeeds.com; 105: CRP; 106 l: KR; 106 r: CRP; 107 l: Pj Aun (S); 107 r: KR; 109 tl: ItsAngela (S); 109 tr: Mateusz Kropiwnicki (S); 109 b: Naaman Abreu (S); 110: KR; 111 tl: Reni PS (S); 111 bl: Kimberly Boyles (S); 111 r: masterpiece creator (S); 114: CRP; 116–127 icons: designed by Freepik from Flaticon.com; 128: Baker Creek Heirloom Seeds/RareSeeds.com; 129: Markus_272 (S); 130: Baker Creek Heirloom Seeds/RareSeeds.com; 131: Pixel-Shot (S); 132: Milaspage (S); 133: Africa Studio (S); 134: PosiNote (S); 135 t: Cora Mueller (S); 135 b: Iaroshenko Maryna (S); 136 l: CRP; 136 r: oksana2010 (S); 137: ChameleonsEye (S); 138: CRP; 139: yuris (S); 140: Baker Creek Heirloom Seeds/RareSeeds.com; 141: Nancy J. Ondra (S); 142: Picture Partners (S); 143: Old Man Stocker (S); 144 t: lzf (S); 144 b: Artem Kontratiev (S); 145: Bubushonok (S); 146 t: pilialoha (S); 146 b: Julitt (S); 147 l: Roxana Scurtu (S); 147 r: EQRoy (S); 148–149: Starikov Pavel (S); 150 l: Contemplar (S); 150 r: S.Myshkovsky (S); 151: ThomasLENNE (S); 152: Olga Miltsova (S); 153: Vineyard Perspective (S); 154 l: CRP; 154 r: CRP; 155 l: CRP; 155 r: CRP; 156 l: KR; 156 r: CRP; 157 l: CowPots.com; 157 r: KR; 158–159 all: KR; 160: KR; 161: CRP; 162: Kathy Jentz, Washington Gardener Magazine, SeedSwapDay.com; 163 tl: KR; 163 bl: KR; 163 r: KR; 165–165: CRP; 166: KR; 167 l: KR; 167 r: CRP; 168–169 all: CRP; 170 l: CRP; 170 r: CRP; 171 l: KR; 171 r: CRP; 172: CRP; 173 t: Krit Leoniz (S); 173 b: wawritto (S); 174: CRP; 175 l: KR; 175 r: Floki (S); 176 tl: Protasov AN (S); 176 tr: Tomasz Klejdysz (S); 176 b: nechaevkon (S); 177 l: Protasov AN (S); 177 r: AnongTH (S); 178 l: KR; 178 m: CRP; 178 r: CRP; 179 tl: KR; 179 tm: CRP; 179 tr: KR; 179 b: CRP; 180 t: KR; 180 b: Ingus Kruklitis (S); 181: CRP; 182 l: KR; 182 r: CRP; 183 l: CRP; 183 r: KR; 184: pilialoha (S); 186: asharkyu (S); 187: Olga Miltsova (S); 188: CRP

Index

Note: Page numbers in *italics* indicate at-a-glance charts of plants' growing needs. Page numbers in **bold** indicate plant profiles.